FML-OSOPHY

FAL-OSOPHY

A Collection of Serious Rhymes

COVER DESIGNED:
SAM Y. MORIS

BY **DR. CB SKELTON**

ReadersMagnet, LLC

Fil-osophy : A Collection of Serious Rhymes
Phool-osophy : A Collection of Humorous Rhymes
Copyright © 2019 by Dr. CB Skelton

Published in the United States of America
ISBN Paperback: 978-1-949981-30-8
ISBN eBook: 978-1-949981-31-5

All rights reserved. No part of this publication may be reproduced, stored in a retrieval system or transmitted in any way by any means, electronic, mechanical, photocopy, recording or otherwise without the prior permission of the author except as provided by USA copyright law.

The opinions expressed by the author are not necessarily those of ReadersMagnet, LLC.

ReadersMagnet, LLC
10620 Treena Street, Suite 230 | San Diego, California, 92131 USA
1.619. 354. 2643 | www.readersmagnet.com

Book design copyright © 2019 by ReadersMagnet, LLC. All rights reserved.
Cover design by Ericka Walker
Interior design by Shemaryl Evans

FIL-OSOPHY

A COLLECTION OF RHYMES ABOUT

SERIOUS SUBJECTS

DEDICATION

God has truly Blessed me by placing female personalities in my life: one mother, six sisters, three wonderful wives (in natural succession) and five cherished biological daughters. Two great stepdaughters, and one daughter-in-law were bonus additions with my second and third marriages. Granddaughters and great granddaughters galore are now completing the picture.

Each has had a part in enhancing my life, causing me to see life's beauty more clearly, discern its philosophical moments more deeply, and appreciate its humorous aspects more fully. Because of their presence, their love, their actions and reactions, life has more meaning, more purpose and more hope.

This book is dedicated to each of the aforementioned,
but especially to the memory of my late first wife.
Nora Louisa Hart Skelton
and of my late second wife,
Hazel Marie "Penny" Morris Skelton

These ladies have inspired, encouraged, consoled, cajoled, loved, cared for and gently driven me. Without them and their Christian faith (which enhanced and encouraged my own faith), my insights and perspectives would be much more limited than they are. My gratitude knows no end.

FOREWORD

I feel much like A Godfather at the birth of *Fil-Osophy/Phool-Osophy*. I know its roots and have watched it slowly develop over the fire-plus years of my close association with its author. Never did I dream a book of poetry would come from any publication where I was in charge. You see, I had an almost ironclad rule against poems in publications owned or managed by me, and there were good reasons for that rule.

First of all, too many people try to write poetry, and too much of the poetry is bad. Then, all of these would-be poets are searching for a place to be published. My fear was that publishing one poem would open a floodgate of submissions (many from my subscribers), most of which would have to be rejected. Rejection of work into which these people have put their heart and soul is difficult for both the publisher and the author.

Only because of our friendship, did I take time to read his submissions when Doctor Skelton brought samples of his work and asked us to try him as a weekly columnist. I knew immediately that he was the exception to my "anti-poetry" rule. His writings were rhythmically metered and rhymed; Some were inspiring, some were touching. Best of all, some were hilariously funny.

From that day forward, I never published a newspaper that did not include one of Doctor Skelton's "rhymes."

He insists they be called "rhymes" instead of "poetry" because he makes no claim of being a poet. I say he can call them whatever he wants, but under any name, they represent some of the best writing it has ever been my privilege to publish, rhyming or not.

As you enter the pages of *Fil-Osophy/Phool-Osophy*, you will find arranged according to subject matter, a few of his rhymed and metered writings that instruct, exhort, reassure and/or entertain. It is my hope they will mean as much to you as they have meant to my subscribers over the years.

Myles Godfrey
Publisher
The Barrow Eagle

CONTENTS

Dedication 7
Foreword 9
Disclaimer 13
I'm Not a Poet 15

Section I : Fil-Osophy or Phool-Osophy 17
Philosophy or "Phool-Osophy" 18

Section II : General Fil-Osophy 19
Philosophy 20
A Changing World 21
Arthur's Philosophy of Life 23
Life Is Like a Symphony 25
Learned from My Window 27
A Lesson from Snowflakes 29
Ode to a Young Man 31
Old Glory Waves 32

Section III : Religious Fil-Osophy 35
Treasures in Earthen Vessels 36
Imperfect Vessels 38
A Triune God 40
In Little Things 42
Sin is Like Kudzu 44
I Witnessed the Power of God Today 47

After the Storm 49
Too Big to Hit 51
Blackie 54

Section IV: Social Fil-Osophy 57
Musings on MLK Day 58
The Right-To-Life Debate 59
The Silent Cry 61
The Big-Bang Theory 63

Section V: Grief Rhymes 67
On Losing a Loved One 68
Helen's Lament 71
Assurance in Sorrow 73
The Coming of Spring 75
Through Tears 77
I Can Ne'er Forget 80
To an Alzheimer's Patient 81
She Is Here 82

Section VI: Professional Fil-Osophy 85
The Nurse 85
A Healer's Prayer 87

DISCLAIMER

To me, poetry has an ethereal quality that is seldom attained. It is not often didactic, rather it usually contains a subliminal message that leaves you wishing for more, while yet probing for its deeper meaning.

My writings do have qualities of rhyme and meter, but they lack sublime, ethereal qualities. They are straightforward and didactic, intended to instruct, inform, and/or entertain. I call my writings strictly "rhymes."

If, after reading, you should choose to call them "Poetry," and me, therefore, "a Poet," I am grateful and honored. In the meantime, I stick with my disclaimer statement,

"I'm Not A Poet."

I'm Not a Poet

I'm not a poet—it's so much worse.
I see the whole wide world in verse.
No. I don't mean it's upside–down
or left is right, and so around.
I think God made this world, and time,
with a sense of meter and of rhyme.
Wherever I look, I plainly see
the handwork of God—His poetry.

I'm not a poet. I can't find words
to set hearts singing like mockingbirds.
It seems when I try to bare my heart
my words don't picture what I want to impart.
Things of great beauty clearly seen in this world,
like a mother and baby or a boy with his girl,
never show clearly in words used by me.
Though they usually rhyme, they're not poetry.

I'm not a poet. As hard as I try,
my words don't warm like a lullaby.
That elusive essence true poets possess
is just that, *elusive*, and I can guess
will continue to escape me 'til the end of time
unless God breathes spirit in my simple rhymes,
causing them to blossom and some soul to bless
with courage and conviction or…just quietness.

I'm not a poet. I'm a rhymer, at best.
Someday, when I stand my final test,
I'll stand before One at the great white throne
to account for the deeds that I have done.
Each thought I've had will be brought to light,
each word I've said, be it wrong or right.
I'll confess to the One who will judge me then,
"I never was a poet. Wish I could have been."

SECTION I

FIL-OSOPHY OR PHOOL-OSOPHY

Philosophy (I distort the word to Phool-osophy for humorous thought) has been defined as "the love or pursuit of wisdom." The wise King, Solomon tells us in the book of Proverbs to seek after wisdom, and he repeats that theme over and over. He also informs us that "a merry heart doeth good like a medicine." (Proverbs 17:22) and, "He that hath a merry heart hath a continual feast.

Phool-osophy is my word for those rhymes designed mostly to entertain. I see no real problem with offering both Fil-osophy and Phool-osophy in the same volume despite James' probing question, doth a fountain send forth in the same place sweet water and bitter?"

There is no designed bitter water here, only desire to make the heart a little more merry and to share a few pearls of wisdom gleaned in more than a half-century dealing with the physical, emotional and spiritual aspects of the health of human beings.

Philosophy or "Phool-Osophy"

I'm a dichotomy! I'll bet you are, too.
I never know which side will show through.
Will it be the deep side some call philosophy?
Or the silly, shallow side I call "phool-osophy?"
It doesn't really matter, for both sides are me!
I'm as much one as the other. I guess, I'll always be.

At one time or other, both sides served me well.
Philosophy has led me to more heights than I can tell;
but "phool-osophy" lifts me from depths when I'm down.
There is nothing more relaxing than acting like a clown.
Just which is the real me, and which the alter-ego?
What makes me click? What really makes me go?

I don't have the answer on the tip of my tongue.
"Phool-osophy" seems evident as when I was young.
But philosophy keeps growing, claims more of my time,
and I'm left to wonder the reason and rhyme?
Do I have to choose one? Or might it just be
that God, Himself, made me a dichotomy?

Solomon, that wise man said, "A time for everything!
For weeping or mourning—for laughter and dancing."
So, perhaps there is reason for a mix of the two,
hoping, at the right time, the right one comes through.
God help the man who no humor ever sees,
And help him who tries to live by just "phool-osophy!"

SECTION II

GENERAL FIL-OSOPHY

(THE AUTHORS PHILOSOPHY, AND THAT SEEN IN OTHERS)

King Solomon, in Proverbs 23:7, said that "as a man thinketh in his heart, so is he." His thoughts and his heart (his philosophy) define how he lives his life, how he relates to his family and rears his children. It is demonstrated in his advice to friends and family, and how he feels about his native land. His very existence is determined by what he thinks in his heart.

The rhymes in this section are general reflections of the author's philosophy of life and/or an attempt to discern and express some of the philosophy seen in the lives of others.

Philosophy
(TO DAVE... A STUDENT OF IT)

A world out there needs change; but I can't change it.
I have neither strength nor mind to rearrange it.
Man's inhumanity to man
is something I don't understand,
But this fact of life remains 'til we constrain it.

I speak to those of you who share my feelings.
There are so many folks who are appealing
to the likes of you and me
who have eyes to clearly see
what the run of history keeps on revealing.

This world is changed not by some great mass movement,
but by one-on-one approach of self-involvement.
I help you ... You help him ...
He, in turn, helps one again.
A chain reaction may begin that brings improvement.

My philosophy of life is not complex.
You must never take life's facts out of context.
You must do the best you can
with whom and what there is at hand.
Then, you simply wait around and see what comes next.

A Changing World

What is this old world coming to
as it persists in changing?
What is a man supposed to do
with all this rearranging?

Who used to be our enemy
has now become our friend.
Who once was broke as he could be
has money now to lend.

What once was taught as absolute
has now become passe;
and the old-fashioned middle route
is called right-wing today.

The virtues—truth and verity—
are long since left behind.
"A handshake is good enough for me!"
Don't let it enter your mind!

Even as the world has changed,
perhaps, I have changed some, too;
Accepting things that once seemed strange
as the proper way to do.

My goals in life remain the same
and the road is straight and narrow.
To reach those goals without cause for shame,
one must shoot straight as an arrow.

I think the proper thing to do
in life until you're dead
is, find a path that is right for you,
and march right on ahead.

Arthur's Philosophy of Life

He was a very good friend of mine
who knew how life should be lived.
"You can only live one day at a time.
What counts most is what you give.

"You've just gotta laugh every chance you get
'cause you're shore gonna get a chance to cry.
A feller thinks better—you can just bet—
when his heart ain't heavy and his eyes are dry.

"There ain't nothing wrong with doing a little work!
Somehow, it gets to be the mark of a man.
Just 'cause you don't know how is no cause to shirk.
Just say, 'I'll try,' and sure nuff, you can.

"When it comes to family, you want to hold 'em close,
but you gotta somehow let 'em know they're free.
When you get a chance to teach 'em, better give the full dose,
'cause they don't spend long a'standing at your knee.

"If you want to have good neighbors, you'd better show 'em how
by doin' things you'd like for them to do
like giving produce from your garden or butter from your cow.
then, pray for 'em! It'll come back to you.

"When the subject is religion, better watch how you talk
'cause you're not just talking 'bout some silly game.
Before you open up your mouth, better think about your walk—
and your walk and talk had better be the same."

Now, he's gone to Heaven. May his memory long remain
to guide those of us who come behind.
His death was our loss, but his LIFE was our gain.
By its light, a better pathway we should find.

Life Is Like a Symphony

Life is like a symphony
you are writing line-by-line.
On some days, you plainly see
a harmony divine.

There will be those dreaded days
filled with discord and strife.
That is just one of many ways
life has of being LIFE.

Life is like a symphony.
Sometimes your spirits soar.
They spur you on with ecstasy
to reach for more, more, more.

Then, as you reach ethereal heights
with tympanic crescendo,
You want to stay, review the sights
and bask in afterglow.

Now, the movement changes and
the mood and pace abate.
You are dragged by unseemly hands
through times and moods you hate.

The Slough of Despond, that awful pit
where we all seem to fall,
Just when you feel consumed by it,
you will see light after all.

Change of movement comes again,
and now the pace is brisk.
More callused now to deal with pain,
you take (or shun) the risks.

Ethereal heights or agony?
You choose how to construct it.
Yes, life is like a symphony!
Now, how will you conduct it?

Learned from My Window

I painted two window frames inside our house.
(A true three-coat painter I'm called hereabout:
one coat on the floor and another on me,
third coat on the window frame, if I get lucky.)

Needless to say, I got paint on the glass.
It needed much cleaning. Alack and alas,
I did what I do best and said, "I will wait
until sometime tomorrow. That won't be too late.

"Besides, it's much easier to scrape when it's dry.
Just watch me, and see how I make that stuff fly."
But, sad to report, my tomorrow never came
And, after six years, there was paint on those panes.

Meanwhile, the front of our house was a mess.
We called a contractor they said is the best.
He came with his crew and they worked just like bees
to clean up the mess. With their work, we were pleased.

The woodwork was painted and shining like new
from ceiling to floor, and the windows shone too—
except those two windows I had never scraped.
That paint shined right through like a big bald-faced ape.

Ashamed of my mess that had been there so long,
I started to scrape with strokes big and strong,
I cleaned off the paint from the glass in the room
Uncovering a fact I would never assume.

Beguiled by the excess of paint I had left there
the painting contractor did not take care.
His job on these windows was strictly third-class.
He left big gobs on his side of the glass.

This lesson I learned and shall never forget:
be careful about the example you set.
Someone might pattern their life after you,
then your mess multiplies by a factor of at least two!

A Lesson from Snowflakes

Snowflakes billow past my window,
each one different—each unique.
Like down that's shaken from a pillow
covering meadow, knoll and peak.

Like a blanket–white–unending;
such great beauty to behold!
Each one different—yet they are blending
in such a way as to bless the soul.

I don't see two snowflakes fighting,
one trying to take another's place.
Each fills his spot—and it's exciting
how the landscape they can grace.

It seems they have an understanding—
No one of them can stand alone.
It's when they're altogether banding
they beautify earth, tree and stone.

How I wish man could learn the lesson
by the snowflakes clearly told;
our differences can be a blessing
to the corporate human soul.

Why should I have to be just like you,
or you try to copy me?
Each one has his own job to do
for the good of society.

Different? Yes! But blended together
with each one doing what he does best,
we need not have to wonder whether
this world can attain true happiness.

Ode to a Young Man

I look at you and I can see POTENTIAL.
I know you have the tools that are essential.
Your body and your mind
are as healthy as you will find,
Yet, somehow, you don't live up to those credentials.

Now is the time when you should be in college,
learn how to earn your own beans and porridge.
Oh, how I wish you would find
the needed frame of mind
To make your soul just hunger after knowledge.

To "just get by" appears your life's ambition.
I have told you that too many times to mention.
But those who travel far
need fuel for their car.
That doesn't come from just your good intentions.

So now, my son, I ask that you remember:
Decisions made in May affect December.
The way you mold your life
will affect your kids and wife—
Not just you—but future family members.

You know full well I am not on your back.
I have always tried to cut you lots of slack.
I promise you, I will pray
each and every day
That God, himself, will get you on the track.

Old Glory Waves

The national debt is astronomic.
The trade deficit is high.
What is the state of our economics?
Is it bust? or boom? and why?

With the ozone, do we still have problems?
Is the globe getting warmer each year?
Does anyone know how we can solve them?
We must deal with them all, I fear.

But Old Glory, our flag, still is waving
from her flagpole high above the square.
And, on our coins, we still are engraving
"In God we trust." See it? Right there!

The streets of our cities are dangerous.
Our children can't go out and play.
Our problem with drugs is cancerous.
You hear of murder every day.

Many wives are victims of violence;
child molesters roam here and there.
The courts give criminals a light sentence,
so they just move elsewhere.

I look up, and can still see Old Glory
and, though I know all is not well,
I have read her hist'ry. She has solved gory
problems and then lived to tell.

The rolls on welfare are quite long,
often covering three generations.
Abuse of all the systems is strong
in every state of our nation.

Taxes are a burden all must bear
to pay the cost of freedom,
a freedom you will not find everywhere.
It is worth the price we pay, and then some!

So, when you see Old Glory in the wind,
her stripes and stars red, white and blue,
just take some time to try and comprehend
how good God has been to you.

You could have been born in some other place
where people have never been free;
and not in these United States
where all enjoy full liberty.

Oh yes, we have some problems we must solve
to right the listing ship of state,
but, if we join hands in deep resolve,
I am certain it is not too late.

As long as Old Glory flies overhead
and our motto stays, "In God we trust,"
and we face those problems we now dread,
our country need not bite the dust

SECTION III

RELIGIOUS FIL-OSOPHY

Every person has a religious philosophy. It may be to deny the very existence of God or to extol the virtues of a particular being. The authors religious conviction is very strong that a triune God created and controls this universe.

God most often shows Himself in very small thing and does most of His work through His creation, though we all are imperfect beings. He is quick to show us that the way to be great is to be a servant to all and to show love for every person regardless of how unlovable they might appear to be.

Sin is a deadly enemy that all of us must try to overcome – not in our own strength – but in the strength that He will supply if only we will ask. By his grace, we may stand through life's many trials.

Treasures in Earthen Vessels
(BASED ON 2 CORINTHIANS 4:7)

A long time ago when the children of Israel
wandered in search of their own Promised Land,
God gave to Moses this great commandment,
"Build me an ark so I can live among men.

And, Moses, I want you to use just the finest,
things that are perfectly pure!
Make all the vessels of gold or silver—
things of great beauty that will ever endure.

But we have these treasures in earthen vessels;
They're vessels not made of silver or gold.
It's so that the Father may get the glory
that in earthen vessels, His Son we behold.

Now you, my friend, may not have much talent,
and you may think you're too young or too old.
But, my God can use every person
who is willing to be used, be he timid or bold.

And, my God will give to you all of the power
that's needed His great work to do.
And then, my friend, may come the glad hour
when you may see God's great work done in you!

For we have these treasures in earthen vessels;
They're vessels not made of silver or gold.
It's so that the Father may get the glory
that in earthen vessels, His Son we behold.
Yes, in earthen vessels, His Son we behold.

Imperfect Vessels

The fact that most Christians will not share their faith
has always been puzzling to me.
Though we're undeserving, we're saved by God's grace
to life everlasting and free.

That ought to be reason to shout from the tree-tops
and tell of His power to forgive.
We should tell the whole world—with hardly a pit-stop
that they, too, might abundantly live.

If someone should give us a cool million dollars,
we'd tell it all over the place.
Of much greater value is the peace that follows
God's gift of salvation by grace.

Yet most of us seemingly try very hard
not to ever let anyone know
that our slate is wiped clean—completely unmarred—
as clean as the new driven snow.

We sit there in silence, with never a word
about how He has borne all our sin,
when we're in the presence of those who've not heard
that they, too, the victory might win.

We talk of the weather—things easily shared—
of our children—what we've done today.
We use lame excuses like, *I'm not prepared.
No one has told me what to say.*

*I'm not a preacher, a teacher or deacon.
I've never attended that class!*
But God's Holy Spirit can shine the right beacon
on our words, though they're stumbling and crass.

Our God has commanded all Christians to witness
as in this world we make our way.
Just tell your own story, though you are scared witless.
His Spirit will guide what you say.

If you were in the desert dying of thirst,
with no way you thought you could win
and found cold, clear water in a slop-jar or worse;
Would it matter what vessel it was in?

Now, we are His vessels—His imperfect vessels—
each scarred by mistakes from the past.
But our God can still use these imperfect vessels,
give life-giving water from a cracked, dirty glass.

A Triune God

To explain a Triune God
is not a simple thing to do.
Most examples seem quite odd
and do not hold completely true
when one puts them to further test.

The sun, with body, light and heat
needs all three parts to function well.
The egg is surely incomplete
without its yellow, white and shell
Of those I've heard, these seem the best.

But do they make an allegory
of a living vibrant entity
that matches with the Bible story
and can relate to folks like me?
or is that link just too absurd?

The Father, Son and Holy Ghost;
the three-in-one or Trinity;
all three comprise the Lord of Hosts,
The Great I Am, the Infinity
according to His holy Word.

Where Jesus said, "I am the <u>vine</u> (John 15; 5)
and you are the branches [of Me]"
is a starting place from the Word Divine
to begin to grasp the Trinity
as being truly one from three.

Picture with me, God as the <u>Root</u>; (Ro 11; 17)
the Spirit as <u>Sap</u> ("fatness" Ro 11; 17 KJV) flowing constantly
from Root through Vine to branch, so fruit
might then be borne abundantly
on grafted branches such as we.

Every plant must have all three—
root, trunk and sap—if it survives.
So every bush or weed you see
as through God's world you walk or drive
should remind you of the Trinity.

God ... truly one; yet, also, three;
Us ... branches grafted to His praise.
Now join with me triumphantly
as heart and voice we gladly raise
in praise to God, blest Trinity.

In Little Things

"Speak to me, God," he said in prayer,
"so I can know you are really there."
The thunder made a powerful sound
and he fell prostrate on the ground.

"Thunder has always made me scared.
Speak to me, God," again he dared.
The wind blew gently through the trees
whose rustling leaves fell in the breeze.

"Oh, no! I will have to rake those up.
Speak to me, God. Come fill my cup!"
A mockingbird trilled, oh, so sweet—
his voice came back filled with defeat,

"Well, God, since You don't choose to speak,
I guess Your touch is what I seek."
A drop of rain fell on his head.
Disgustedly, he turned and said,

"Why don't You choose to answer yet?
Please, touch me now, before I'm wet."
A butterfly flew toward his eye
and brushed his cheek as it passed by.

"That doggone bug flew right at me,"
He said as he refused to see
the touch of God or hear His voice
since God had made a different choice

than, in his mind, he had expected.
Sadly, he left—nor yet suspected
he had heard God's voice and felt His touch
in little things that don't count much.

Sin is Like Kudzu

Sin is like Kudzu in so many ways.
Both seem to be there with from cradle to grave.
That neither of them was made by God
is an arguable fact, and may seem quite odd.
What does seem true, nevertheless,
is He made both possible. Man did the rest!

I have heard Kudzu is only a hybrid—
was not included in things God created.
So it is with sin—God never said
one should beat another until he was dead.
He made us free agents to make our own choice
and we listened to Satan's instead of God's voice.

Kudzu is a model of well-thought-out wrong choices
about which one seldom if ever rejoices.
Developed in the Orient—imported by man
to help stop erosion of soil from the land.
Well, it did its job—but so much more, brother,—
as it usurped the land from one shore to another.

Sin takes over like Kudzu, if given full rein.
You do the same sin now and over again.
The more you repeat it, it's easier to do.
Other sins follow, and then, sin has you.
Next thing you know, it claims family and friend,
then the cycle repeats, it seems, without end.

Kudzu appears a young, tender, green shoot
that just look so harmless, you don't "give a hoot"
if it wraps right around the base of your tree.
"It's just so pretty! What harm could there be?"
Soon, shoots that were tender are hardened like iron
and life starts to choke out by the tightening vine.

The same thing with sin. At first, it's exciting;
so innocent appearing; so downright inviting.
You think, "Such a thing could not control me.
I can just play around. I'll be cool as can be."
Then, before you can reckon, you're completely entwined
and, just like with Kudzu, you're caught in the vine.

You can cut all Kudzu vines down to the ground
and think you have stopped it. Then just turn around,
it is growing like crazy and climbing a tree.
The same way with sin. When you come off a spree,
you swear you will not do that thing any more—
then find yourself doing the sin as before.

The roots of the Kudzu dig deep in the ground,
and if roots are left, Kudzu will be found.
To be rid of Kudzu, one must kill every root
by digging or poison or by cutting every shoot
again and again 'til it bleeds to its death.
And sins roots will stay 'til you draw your last breath

Unless, by the might of some power divine,
you are freed from the grip of sin's terrible vine,
sin surely will continue to grow and abound
'til, in spiritual death, you are laid in the ground.
For, as surely as Kudzu brings death to your tree,
unforgiven sin will bring death—eternally!

Surely, you'll allow me just one stanza more
to bring to a head things I have said before,
to wit, "Though the sin root is still part of me,
it need not destroy me, as Kudzu will a tree.
Jesus came to earth to save us from sin.
By repentance and accepting Him, new life we'll begin.

I Witnessed the Power of God Today

I witnessed the power of God today, in many different ways.
I know He is a living God who hears us when we pray.
But He is so much more than that! He wants to fill our days
with deeds of joy and goodness, so we'll give to Him all praise.
His power, mercy and His might in many things abound.
You, too, may know His power if you'll only look around.

I witnessed the power of God today in a rushing waterfall.
Only He could make the mountain that stood so very tall
and the stream of running water that rose from its inner depths
then hurried to the point from which it looked as if it leapt.
I saw the power of my God through eyes He gave to me.
And so I said, "I thank you, God, for allowing me to see!"

I witnessed the power of God today in the cooing of a dove.
He spoke sweetly to his mate. He seemed to speak of love.
When such a great emotion in earth's nature realm is shown,
it serves to bring remembrance that our God is on His throne.
I heard the power of my God through His wondrous gift of ears.
And so I said, "I thank you, God, for ability to hear!"

I witnessed the power of God today in a fragrant blooming rose.
It completely warmed my being as I held it to my nose.
How can a thing of beauty have an odor so divine?
Answers to questions of this sort are simple to a God like mine.
I sensed the power of my God through His gift of smell.
And so I said, "I thank you, God, for this wondrous gift as well!"

I witnessed the power of God today in warming rays of sun.
It felt so good to know those wintry days had come and gone.
I'm told He simply spoke the words and said, "Now let there be!"
And earth and sun came to exist for all eternity.
I sensed the power of my God through His gifts of feel and touch.
And then I said, "I'm grateful, God! You've given me so much."

I witnessed the power of God today in tangy, tasty fruit.
He made several different ones, my different moods to suit.
How each has its distinctive flavor, I'll never understand,
but the foolishness of God is wiser than the wisest man.
I witnessed the power of my God in the miracle of taste.
And so I said, "I praise you, God, for this sign of your embrace."

I witnessed the power of God today in calmness of my heart.
Such a quiet and peaceful feeling, only my God could impart.
I did not see nor hear nor smell. I did not touch or taste.
It was like a sixth sense, and it comes about through faith.
By faith, the power of my God now resides in me!
All I can say is, "Thank you, God! All praise be unto Thee!"

After the Storm

When I first saw the tree, I knew quite well
why its owner chose to leave it there.
Tall, straight and green… like a magic spell
its long lacy limbs embraced the air.
After the monsoon rains that fell,
the greener tree seemed much more fair.

Then, without warning, came the storm
with mighty, boisterous, gale-force winds.
They shook the tree out of shape and form.
Each time it swayed threatened its end.
Its shallow roots—great for the norm—
in this storm could not hold within.

I saw the tree just lying there,
a helpless, broken, dying thing.
Its roots, exposed to sun and air,
could not support or nurture bring.
A thing of beauty, oh so rare,
uprooted in one final fling.

This raised the question of my roots…
how deep, how firmly are they grown?
And are they set in gospel truth
of Jesus Christ—and Christ alone?
Or do I put Him in some booth
and place myself upon the throne?

Rough storms of life will surely come
 to test the base foundation
laid for each and every one
of us… and of our nation.
Lord, in the storm, (and when it's done,)
may our roots firmly hold their stations.

Anchored in your perfect love,
Lord, I pray You'll help me stand
with strength that comes from God above,
who gently guides and holds my hand,
until my spirit like a dove
soars off to You in Beulah-land.

Too Big to Hit

David, a bright young man, came to the battle-field
bringing food for his brothers who were far from home.
Imagine David's deep, dark sorrow as his sight revealed
God's army bogged down—still as any stone.

David saw a giant of a man—a mighty Philistine—
parade before God's army in full array.
His daily ranting, raving sounded mighty mean
saying, "Men of Israel, why will you die today?

"Send out now your champion—the two of us will fight.
If he kills me, then we will be your slaves.
If I kill him, then serve us. That is fair and right!
Why will you die, when your lives can be saved?"

At the sight of this great giant, Israel's army cringed in fear.
Not one of Israel's men would call his bluff.
Said David to Saul, " I once killed a lion and bear.
God will help me slay him. He's not that tough.

Who does he think he is, uncircumcised Philistine,
to defy the army of the Living God?"
Saul said, "You're such a young man—just in your teens.
He'll strike you dead—lay you beneath the sod."

David replied, "I do not fear the slightest bit.
God will be with me in a time like this.
Your fearful soldiers think, 'He's too big to hit'.
I'm here to say, "He's far too big to miss!"

Laying aside the armor Saul gave him,
David chose out from the brook, five round, smooth stones.
With only slingshot in hand, this lad, small and slim,
strode boldly toward the giant. He appeared to be alone.

"Am I a dog that a boy with a stick brings me down?"
Goliath roared, "I'll feed you to the birds of the air!"
"Not by sword but by God's Spirit is salvation found,"
David sang as he rushed to meet Goliath there.

A single stone in his slingshot, whirled round and round.
when turned loose, the stone flew with a steady hiss.
The stone stuck in his forehead, Goliath fell to the ground.
David thought, "You see, he was too big to miss!"

You or I may have a problem that appears a giant
and keeps us from achieving goals in life.
It may cause us to shirk or not be self-reliant—
not be the proper husband, child or wife.

*We may, like the ostrich, stick our heads in sand
as we hope and pray the problem goes away.
We may turn tail and run to beat the band
think we will face that problem another day.*

*We should face our problems like David—never quit!
March straight toward that yawning, deep abyss.
Ask God for strength and courage. It's not too big to hit!
With God's help, it will be too big to miss!*

Blackie

Blackie was a Spanish mule
that could make me feel like a stupid fool
by raising in me such intense ire,
that I felt in danger of hell-fire.

I found myself using all those bad words—
you know, the ones I had often heard
those other boys use on the school yard
back in those days when times were so hard.

Of course, none of this was ever my fault!
I was plowing a mule not worth her salt,
and she aggravated me every day.
It was her fault I spoke that way.

My Daddy would say when he came in late,
"The lines you plow are not very straight."
"Daddy, that mule can aggravate,"
I would say (and I was only eight).

August came, and with it Revival,
and I needed help for my survival.
I walked the aisle, gave the preacher my hand,
and got my ticket for the Promised Land.

Next morning, as I hooked her to the plow,
I said, "Blackie, I'm a Christian now,
and those words I've been saying every day—
I'm not going to talk to you that way."

Before, in that field, we had gone two roundabouts,
every one of those words had already come out.
The halo I had worn so auspiciously
had fallen around my neck and was choking me.

Nothing has changed, old Satan seemed to say,
you're the same sorry thing you were yesterday!
And they had told me that nothing could sever
me from salvation forever and ever.

But that was before I knew Philippians 1:6,
a biblical promise on which my mind fixed:
He who began a good work (in your life)
will be faithful to complete it 'til the day of Christ.

So, Blackie, I owe a debt to you.
You helped me to find One who has been true
and led me for years–but obviously—
He is not done. He's still working on me!

SECTION IV

SOCIAL FIL-OSOPHY

In every society, issues arise where there are differences of opinion. The person who is a writer is not excluded from having an opinion or conclusion on these issues. He is, in fact, expected to voice an opinion or conclusion after giving the matter careful study.

This author has strong right-to-life opinions as well as opinions on evolution and the decency of humankind. Some of these opinions are expressed in the rhymes in this following section

Musings on MLK Day

What is the truest measurement of a man?
Surely, it is not the color of one's skin.
A higher plane we seek;
a view from loftier peak
that may require that some begin again.

The time is here when you and I must see
a person's measure is ability—
not sex or race or creed,
but can (s)he fill a need
to help us as we serve humanity?

Young Martin Luther King once had a dream
where, in his mind, he saw an endless stream
of folks from every race
each filling his own place
to help to bring to pass this heavenly theme.

All humanity should share this common goal,
and join in his vision heart and soul.
To others you must do
as you'd have them do to you,
is a motto that should bring things under control.

It matters not what color, sex or creed,
we must unite to help all those in need.
Then we fulfill the thesis
as stated first by Jesus,
More blest it is to give than to receive.

The Right-To-Life Debate

Abortion rights are debated today,
the object of passion and study.
There are those who say, "There is just no way
you can say what to do with *my* body!"

Others will answer, "That's a life within you,
and you have no right to end it.
God placed life there, and you know it's true.
It's my Christian duty to defend it!"

Another debate that goes on and on
is about what we call Euthanasia.
Dr. Kervorkian has fought for and won
the right to play Lord and Savior.

The rule of that court was: It now is all right
to end life for "humanitarian" reasons.
We now can play God, decide to end life!
On the aged, it is now open season.

With such disregard for life at its start
and, again, near its setting of sun,
Is it any surprise that we tend to impart
disregard for the life of anyone?

Murder and torture are natural offshoots
of society where life is thought cheap.
Is it a great wonder America bears fruit
with bodies thrown on the trash-heap?

Man has always wished to play God—
It was his first great temptation.
Satan said, "Eat fruit! Be wise like God!"
Since then, man has needed salvation.

Life is a precious, God-given thing
to never be lightly regarded
from its inception in Mother's womb
'til, by natural death, we are parted.

The Silent Cry

Who will stand for me?
I cannot stand alone.
Who will speak for me?
I have no voice of my own.
How have I offended
to now be put to death?
Why must my life be ended
before I ever draw a breath?

From its uterine prison walls
there comes the silent cry,
Will somebody hear my call?
I do not wish to die!
Surely, there is someone
who could love a child like me;
who would like someday to see me run,
or maybe climb a tree.

Who will stand for me?
I cannot stand alone.
Who will speak for me?
I have no voice of my own.
How have I offended
to now be put to death?
Why must my life be ended
before I ever draw a breath?

What is life? I ask of you
why don't I qualify?
My heart beats just like yours do.
I even sometimes cry!
You can trace my brain waves;
I feel things just like you.
Yet, they come at me with stainless blade
and tear my flesh in two.

Who will stand for me?
I cannot stand alone.
Who will speak for me?
I have no voice of my own.
How have I offended
to now be put two death?
Why must my life be ended
before I ever draw a breath?

Will YOU stand for me?

Will YOU speak for me?

Will YOU stand and speak for me?

The Big-Bang Theory

I have heard it over and over again
'til I have become quite weary,
this product of some modern brain
they call the Big-Bang theory.

It seems, as you hear the scientists:
space, at first, was completely empty!
Then, <u>by chance</u>, there came to exist
a very small particle of energy

which, by a process they do not understand,
suddenly reacted in such a way
as to form the sky, sea and land,
the moon for night and sun for day.

For eons and eons and eons of time,
ever expanding in time and in space,
this matter continued <u>*with reason and rhyme*</u>
until everything found its own proper place.

After millions and billions of years, they tell,
with only chance as guide and stay,
there emerged one small single cell;
and, from that, mankind was on his way.

Through amoebae and fishes—through tadpole and frog
ever evolving to a *more complex* state,
eventually there rose up out of the bog
a four-legged being, whose ultimate fate

is more evolution through mouse, rat and weasel,
by mere chance, over thousands of years,
<u>*Not by a plan on some great artist's easel,*</u>
through monkey and ape, man finally appears.

This consummate being... this great work of art
who, through his great mind and strong will
can travel in space and can transplant a heart...
came <u>*without plan and from nil?*</u>

It seems to me it takes much more faith
to swallow a tale such is this
than it takes to believe that God did create
both earth and man, as claimed in Genesis.

I would rather think that the bit of energy
that the Big-Bang theory extols
is the *mighty word of God* as He said, "Let there be!"
and the universe starts to unfold.

A strong guiding hand through the eons of time
and a well-thought-out, grand master-plan
are surely indicated by the reason and rhyme
of nature and the grand creation—man.

Science speaks so loudly of a power on high
who formed balanced sea, sky and sod.
Why is it that scientists continue to deny
the existence of the creator, my God?

SECTION V

GRIEF RHYMES

There is no time in life when poetry is more greatly appreciated than in times of grief. The times are very infrequent when you attend a friend or loved one's funeral and not hear some type of poetry either read or sung. The rhythmic flow of soothing words seems somehow to act as a healing balm.

The following poems, written by this author, have been frequently used for consolation and/or advice at times when his patients, friends or family were in grief situations.

On Losing a Loved One

What can I say? What can I do?
At least I can pray and say, "I love you."
But, that won't stop the pain or fill that place,
So I say once again, I pray for God's grace.

Jesus wept to show His pain
as His friend, Lazarus, lay in death,
knowing well he'd rise again.
Himself would give him second breath!

Why did He cry those royal tears …
He, the Lord of love and bliss?
I think to show us that our tears
are normal at a time like this.

There is a proper time for tears
and you must let them freely flow.
When you have had someone for years,
it is quite hard to let them go.

So, cry as long as there is need,
for death has entered in your door.
The time will come when you should heed
the call for you to cry no more.

A loved one's death brings great despair:
the whole world seems as black as night.
But, death is nothing when compared
to that LIFE lived in our sight.

So, this instruction I give you
as you travel the road ahead:
Remember—as soon as you dare to—
the LIFE of your loved one, now dead.

Death wins a victory when it causes
its victim's LIFE to be forgot.
LIFE calls for memories and applauses.
Death most assuredly does not!

Each LIFE is its own grand memorial
to celebrate long after it's done.
Death is just the end of earthly trails;
the time the final race is won.

Can one be dead who lives in memory?
...is spoken of in love from time to time?
The memorial of LIFE is not death—believe me:
Remembering is that LIFE's best shrine.

You must recall good times spent together;
times when you "got in each other's hair;"
Times there were storms you had to weather;
Times things were bleak; the cupboard bare.

When, with a heart that's filled with love,
you can recall these memories
of your loved one who's gone above,
Death is robbed of its victory.

Helen's Lament
(A RONDEAU REDOUBLE FOR HELEN MCDANIEL WHOSE HUSBAND WAS KILLED IN FRANCE IN 1944)

Brief! So brief the hours we tasted love:
just ten days to share our wedded bliss
matched by God who reigns in Heav'n above.
Long! So long the years to savor this.

I was young when we shared our first kiss.
We were like the lark who found the dove
never dreaming things would go amiss.
Brief! So brief the hours we tasted love.

Soldier husband—polished boot and glove;
his appointment he could not dismiss
when they came, his orders from above.
Just ten days to share our wedded bliss.

In my heart, I was assured of this,
he would always be my turtledove.
There's no doubt we came to this abyss
matched by God who reigns in Heav'n above.

He wrote letters telling of his love,
how he longed to share again my kiss
and the warmth of his own ladylove.
Long! So long the years to savor this.

Hitler's men, the worldwide nemesis,
took the life of my dear turtledove.
I, of all the world, would be remiss
should I e'er forget that wondrous love!

Brief! So, brief the hours.

Assurance in Sorrow

I used to be so very sure
that I could win the race;
that I could evermore endure—
keep up this load and pace.

But, now that (s)he has gone away,
I don't know what I'll do.
Lord Jesus, I can only pray
You'll keep me close to You.

I don't know why (s)he had to go.
I just don't understand.
Just this—and this alone—I know,
that You will hold my hand.

You'll lead me on a path that's straight.
You'll lift me when I fall.
You'll bring me through that narrow gate.
You'll be my all-in-all.

Slow, so slowly, comes the light
of new day that's a'borning.
Weeping endures but for the night,
but joy comes in the morning.

So, Jesus, with my faith in You
and counting on Your strength,
my Christian journey I'll pursue
no matter what its length.

Then, some day in a better place
called Heaven's Golden Shore,
we'll be together, face-to-face,
the three of us once more.

Even so, come quickly, Lord Jesus.

The Coming of Spring

I see you there, you little squirrel,
running so fast with your tail unfurled.
Why in the world are you in such a hurry?
Why all the hustle and bustle and scurry?
Oh, I see her now—she's a cute little thing!
You chase a girl because it's coming up Spring.

Hello there, little yellow jonquil,
peeping through the sod on the side of the hill.
It is hard to believe that your Winter's nap is done
and you are called to awaken by the warmth of the sun.
Such beautiful things the warming sun does bring.
You're one of the wonders of the coming of Spring.

I hear you well, you little brown bird,
singing and chirping as if you must be heard.
I see you are carrying another piece of straw
for building your nest after cold Winter's thaw.
Of course, little bird, I know why you sing.
You are praising God for the coming of Spring.

And I, though my spirit is sometimes low,
know in my heart what the whole world should know—
that God, in His wisdom, has a great plan
not always understood by the mere mind of man.
He has perfect control of everything,
and after the Winter, there always comes Spring.

Now Winter is here and I see dim through tears
for the loss of the mate that I had all those years.
She has gone to a place that is better by far
than this beautiful world where you and I are.
Then, some day, He will take me on bright angel's wings.
I will see her again at the coming of Spring.

Through Tears

The dirt is red and oh so soft
and smells so sweet and fresh.
The sky is blue as I look aloft
while the sun sets in the West.

The fragrant flowers she loved so well
adorn the place where she is lying.
The dirt is red and—I am sure you can tell—
so are my eyes from much crying.

The dirt is wet and there is no sod—
oh, it is sinking there at the corner.
I know it is wet from the tears of God
as He looks down on this mourner.

The wilting flowers rustle a bit
in response to the breeze that is blowing.
The dirt is wet and I wonder as I sit:
Why must my tears keep on flowing?

The sod is brown where they put it back
to cover the place where she is lying.
The fading flowers—their leaves turned black—
thrown away because they were dying.

The clouds are dark and the skies so gray
and I am sure it soon will be storming.
The sod is brown, and I kneel and pray
as hot tears my cold cheeks are warming.

The grass is now green where she is laid to rest
and I can hear birds sweetly singing.
The flowers seem to want to look their best;
in the distance, church chimes are ringing.

The fluffy white clouds in the sky up above
look like sheep in a verdant blue pasture.
The grass is green and—though I rest in His love—
tears flow because I still miss her.

"Death is a debt every person must pay,"
people say with a heart full of feeling.
"Time is a healer of all things," they say,
and I am in need of a healing.

Slowly—so slowly each inch seems a mile—
I am working my way through this jungle,
and, ever so often, I think with a smile
I see light at the end of the tunnel.

God, in His wisdom, is trying to teach me
a lesson of real faith and trust.
And I, though I stumble, must let him reach me
to help me adapt and adjust.

His peace and His strength He is wanting to give
to me for the living of life
and, somehow, the message in how I must live
required that He take my dear wife.

So, God, as I struggle through times that are rough
and days that are filled with despair,
help me remember—and know it is enough—
that You are in charge and You care!

And, just like her gravesite—first red and now green
with beautiful, deep-rooted sod—
my life is being groomed by a power unseen—
the strong, mighty hand of my God.

I Can Ne'er Forget
(A TUNE TEXT)

Sometimes, when my troubles get me down,
Tears flow 'til I think I'll nearly drown—
I remember all things work together for the good
for those called for the purpose of the Lord
        and
I can ne'er forget that Jesus saves.
I can ne'er forget He's on His throne.
I can ne'er forget He's in control of everything
and I can ne'er forget I am His own.

Dark and dreary clouds may hide my way
and I cannot see the light of day.
I remember Jesus is the only source of light
and my soul is precious in His sight
        and
I can ne'er forget that Jesus saves.
I can ne'er forget He's on His throne.
I can ne'er forget He's in control of everything
and I can ne'er forget I am His own.

Through the valley of the shadow I have come
and it seems I'll never find my home.
I remember, God, Himself, is still my Shepherd true
and I know He'll safely see me through
        and
I can ne'er forget that Jesus saves.
I can ne'er forget He's on His throne.
I can ne'er forget He's in control of everything
and I can ne'er forget I am His own.

To an Alzheimer's Patient
(WRITTEN AFTER OBSERVING A VISIT OF AN ALZHEIMER'S PATIENT BY A LOVED ONE)

I stood by your bedside unrecognized
by you, whose mind had always been keen.
You looked straight at me—nothing in your eyes;
no love, joy—or hatred—could be seen.
I told you I loved you—and it came from my heart—
those words shared so often in the past.
It is not a one-way love. We were too close to part.
but some things are too good to last.

Your wasted body lay folded like a knife—
no movement from head down to toe.
The motion of breathing, your only sign of life.
Why must it be? I will never know.
Why imprison a soul in a body not fit?
Why a mind fade before life is done?
Why to the good and the bad not hurt a bit?
I have no answers! Does anyone?

I spoke of things we always talked about.
There was no sign you heard a single word!
But, I kept on talking, for I must never doubt
that the language of love will be heard.
A love not returned is the hardest of all—
and I swore I would love you until death.
I still pray for healing. Should God not hear my call,
I will be here for as long as we have breath!

She Is Here

I opened the door to my home so dear,
(it was so much like a dream.)
"Go away! Go away! She is not here,"
it seemed I heard my house scream.

Sadly, I turned and started to go—
wondering where it might be—
To whom can I turn? Where could I go
since she is not here with me?

Then came the thought so strong in my mind,
Get back to where you belong!
I never promised this life would be kind,
filled with nothing but sunshine and song.

I never promised roads that were smooth;
I felt the wind and all its chill.
You know I was spat on, rejected and bruised
when I walked up Calvary's hill.

Now, you go back and get in your place
and do what I called you to do.
<u>*Nobody is served by the slack in your trace,*</u>
<u>*but I will be forever with you.*</u>

So, I turned around and opened the door,
assured of <u>His</u> presence with me.
Then, from the ceiling down to the floor,
my darling wife I could see!

I looked at pictures often seen before
of her and the children she bore.
In each one of them I was certain and sure—
<u>She is here!</u> She is here forevermore!

SECTION VI

PROFESSIONAL FIL-OSOPHY

The Nurse

In times of great sorrow and trouble
when things seem so tense and so terse,
who's there to help on the double?
Your "angel of mercy," the Nurse.

When babies are in need of a'borning,
each pain seems to get worse and worse.
Who sits there from night until morning
to aid the birth process? The Nurse.

When fever and illness are raging;
when things seem to go in reverse
for those who are young—or the aging,
who tries to upright them? The Nurse.

For such times, the right mode of treatment
she has taken great pains to rehearse.
Thank God for this depth of commitment
from this unheralded worker, the Nurse.

She studied quite hard for her title—
can quote you "both chapter and verse".
Now join me in this glad recital
of great praise and honor to the Nurse.

Oh persons of such love and caring—
our helpers from cradle to hearse—
forgive us when we fail in sharing
our love and respect for you, Nurse.

A Healer's Prayer

Oh God, who by Thy Word unfurled
this universe with our own world;
Who did all natural laws reveal
which we now use in our quest to heal.

We humbly come to seek Thy face
and pray for wisdom, love and grace.
That we go about our healing task
imbued with Thy strength is all we ask.

Help us to feel our patient's pain
and embrace his desire to be well again.
May we empathize with husband or wife
as their mate for years fights for his/her life,

and yet not be so emotionally involved
we're blinded to problems that must be solved.
May our minds and our eyes be so sharp, so keen
nothing escapes that should be known or seen.

May our constant study keep us abreast
of the new and old, to know what is best.
May You give to us the strength and will
to press right on in our quest to heal.

And as we stand by our patient's side
we ask that You will be our guide;
and give us the wisdom to clearly see,
the source of all healing comes from Thee.
Amen

My Wife and My Girlfriend

My wife and my girlfriend met face to face
one morning early this week.
I wasn't worried. It's quite commonplace,
but my girlfriend never will speak.

My wife took one look, said, "Your hair is a mess!"
My girlfriend made no reply.
She doesn't want to cause trouble, I guess,
and I can appreciate why.

My wife looked again and said, "You're getting fat
and really should go on a diet."
My girlfriend once more answered nothing to that
and still remained perfectly quiet.

Of wrinkles and double chins my wife chattered on.
I smiled as I watched through the crack.
Knowing full well they were not there alone,
my girlfriend simply smiled back.

Then, from the mirror, my wife turned aside
to start with the tasks of the day;
And, like a shadow at perfect noontide,
my girlfriend just faded away.

In shock and horror, she said to her child,
"Don't kiss that canary! Please!
You just might catch something wild!
You could catch a canareal disease.

The little girl, seeming perfectly at ease,
said, "We're a combination unbeatable.
I'm not worried about canareal disease,
'cause I know, if I get it, it's TWEETABLE!

Kiss My Canary

The little girl loved her canary—
would take him everywhere.
In July or January,
he might be sitting in her hair.

She loved to hear his sweet singing
and to watch his graceful flight.
It was a cause for tear bringing
to cover his cage for the night.

Her mother didn't like that bird! Indeed!
It drove her almost to despair
to find a yellow feather or a bird-seed
on the fabric of her best arm-chair.

God only knows about that 'fruitloop'
and what action she might take
if she ever found one trace of bird-poop
on the hem of her living room drape.

One day, Mom working in her kitchen
saw an action she thought absurd—
her flesh and blood daughter was kissing
that dirty, little, yellow bird!

The guide then led Tom Selleck and me
to a room and a woman like the first.
"Tom Selleck," he said, "here you'll spend eternity
to pay for your sins while on earth."

Far down the long hallway, the guide then led me
to a room that was spacious and bright,
with drapes as pretty as could possibly be,
and shadowless, natural light.
There were soothing pastels that could turn any head;
the view was an eye-popping show.
And, there on a soft, warm and comfortable bed
sat beautiful Marilyn Monroe.

The guide turned from me and looked at Marilyn
as he said with apparent chagrin,
"My dear, you must spend eternity with him
to pay for your earthly sin."

Cruel and Unusual Punishment

The plane crashed into the mountainside
in my dream that was real as could be.
Thank God, there were just three folks who died,
Tom Cruise, Tom Selleck and me.
Together we showed at the judgment bar,
Tom Cruise, Tom Selleck and me.
The keeper said, "You're together thus far,
now come follow me, you three."

We followed him in a long narrow hallway,
Tom Cruise, Tom Selleck and me.
Until he opened and stood in the doorway
of a room that was awful to see.
The walls were jet black. It was small, without view;
the furniture black, with no pad.
One beam of dim light shined unsteadily through,
and no creature comforts it had.

The ugliest woman I ever did see
was crouched there without signs of mirth.
Our guide said, Tom Cruise, here you'll spend eternity
to pay for your sins while on earth."

In His wisdom, God stuffed His servant's nose
with the pollen allergies of Spring.
Our patient might well have smelled like a rose,
our preacher could not smell one thing!

He had missed his dinner to come to this place,
after having already missed lunch.
His stomach felt like a wide-open space.
He needed food! Now! A whole bunch!

There on the table at the patient's bedside
was a beautiful sight to behold.
Peanuts! Our pastor's eyes opened wide.
They more than half filled the bowl.

As he continued his pastoral visit,
he picked up a peanut or two.
Then he found he simply could not quit
before all the peanuts were through.

"My goodness! I've eaten all your peanuts!"
He said in shock and dismay.
"Never before have I done such
a thing as I've done here, today!"

"That's okay, Preacher," came the patient's reply,
"they're so hard and there ain't no way to soften.
About all I can do, as hard as I try,
is to suck all the chocolate off 'em!"

A Pastoral Visit

The old man lay in his hospital bed
fighting a fight for his life.
He had little chance, somebody said,
so downhearted since losing his wife.

He never bathed anymore, it seemed.
His aroma was heavy in the air.
Tobacco juice flowed in an ongoing stream
down his chin, as he just lay there.

There was one solitary tooth in his head
which he kept for reasons unknown.
He spent almost all of his time in the bed—
just lying there—all alone.

No friends ever came to sit by his side—
no family to show that they cared.
The odor—like one who had already died—
kept away most who would have dared.

It was into this scene his minister came,
a young man with strong will like iron.
Not to have come would have put him to shame
and come short of his God's great design.

One fact of life that truly does hurt
is stressed spelled backward makes desserts.
With stress a big part of this life,
you can spread it thin with a dessert knife.

But, stick to your diet and exercise
and you'll soon be back to your proper size.
I gave up my jogging—not for lack of desire—
my thighs rubbed together and set my shorts on fire.

On Losing the Weight Battle

Blessed are those who hunger and thirst
and toil and strain—or even worse.
Surely the Lord will lead them out,
if they can only stay with the diet.

I watch them as they go jogging by
or walk on feet that are trying to fly.
I hear them as they grunt and groan
in pairs or groups—sometimes alone.
They speak of things I really hate
like, "I've just got to lose some weight!"

It is a shock when one realizes
a suit in a closet soon shrinks two sizes
and one pound of candy grows five pounds of fat.
These people and I are dealing with that.

Inside each fat person, some say without doubt,
resides a thin person who wants to get out.
But don't let him grieve you or cause you heart-ache!
You can sedate him with one chocolate cake.

I'll swear, and you can mark my word,
I eat just like a humming-bird;
Of course (the avian scientists say)
they eat three times their weight in a day.

The Power of Scripture
(BASED ON A STORY FROM THE INTERNET)

The old lady returned home after prayer-meeting
with no thought of having the unwanted greeting
of a burglar caught red-handed and face to face.
She said a quick prayer and asked God for grace.
"Acts 2; 38!" she yelled to the thief.
('Repent and be baptized,' it says if you are brief.)

To her great surprise, the thief stopped in his tracks
without ever bothering to even look back.
She lifted the phone and dialed 911,
completely amazed at what scripture had done.

Soon came the Police to take custody
of the thief, who just stood there not trying to flee.
They read him his rights and put on the handcuffs.
He gave them no cause for treating him rough.

Then came the questions. They asked him his name
and from what state and what city he came.
They asked how he got in that poor lady's door
and if he was ever arrested before.
One of the questions they asked him for sure
was, "Why did you stop when she quoted scripture?"

"Quoted me scripture," he gasped in dismay,
"I didn't hear nothing that sounded that way!
She told me clear—and my hearing is great—
she had an axe and had two Thirty-eights."

A Friend in Your Need
IS A FRIEND INDEED

"I will be there when you need me,"
was his promise to his uncle.
"All you have to do is call me,
I will board the closest vehicle.

"If you are broke and need some money,
for a small loan you might hanker;
Just so quick it won't be funny,
I will be there with my banker.

"If you are down with rheumatism
and you need a pill concocter,
Before you rub on all that jism,
I will be there with my doctor.

"If your clothes are all so threadbare
that you fear the great unveiler,
You must call me—don't just stand there.
I will be there with my tailor.

"If you have some legal trouble—
more than just those two-bit messes—
I will be there on the double,
and I'll bring two great eye-witnesses."

She emailed five close friends of Lindstrom
inquiring if he were their guest?
By noon, five emails had in come
each simply answering, "yes."

Lindstrom's True Friends

Lindstrom was quite a philanderer,
and getting worse all the time.
His wife worried about this wanderer
but could not watch him full-time.

Each night she cruised all the barrooms
trying to check on her mate.
After she slept in her bedroom,
Lindstrom would come home quite late.

She hired a good private detective
in hopes he could give her some leads.
His work on this case was defective
with more talk than productive deeds.

Meanwhile, the hours of Lindstrom
got later and later each night.
He'd be out past midnight, and then some
until it was too late to fight.

When one night had turned to wee morning,
and Lindstrom failed yet to come home
without one prior word of warning,
frustration made her feel alone.

My outfield play was equally as good,
with catches that were nothing short of great.
If someone tried to score from third, I would
simply throw him out at home plate!

Major leagues franchises and their scouts
beat a well-worn path to my door.
I could sign with any team, without a doubt!
Each one offered more, more and more.

Every one wanted my name on the line.
One said, "I'll give ten million bucks!"
Just as I started the contract to sign
darned if I didn't wake up!
(p.s. I was equally good in other sports in my dreams.)

The Complete Ballplayer

I wish you could have seen me as a child
when playing in a baseball game.
Those who saw me went completely wild
when up to the plate I came.

An air of excitement hushed the crowd
as at the whistling ball I swung.
Then as their cheers became even more loud,
the ball took off; fast, straight and long.

Each swing would make the ball fly out the park,
or at least to the base of the fence.
Should one be caught, it would be quite a shock
and then the crowd cheered the defense.

When I peered threatening from the pitcher's mound,
those batters shook hard at their knees.
Most often they swung at just the sound
or, sometimes, in pure fright they'd freeze.

No one could ever really hit the ball,
except for a pop-up now and then.
and when they swung and hit nothing at all,
they'd never want to face me again.

We'll put a tub inside the thing
of porcelain that's white,
with running water—like a spring—
just the thing for Saturday night.

And yonder on that farthest wall
(if it's within our power)
we'll hang the most modern thing of all—
we'll hang the Parson's shower.

And no one needs to see him
when he's bathing—that's for certain—
so, we'll hang this little metal ring
to hold a shower curtain.

And underneath the staircase,
where it's gettin' kinda short,
we'll put the wonder of the age—
a toilet of some sort.

Don't worry 'bout the Preacher,
he's chief Bulldog in this town,
and he won't need a teacher
to know how to hunker down.

And so, for many, many, many years
(don't do one thing to spoil it)
I've served quite well through smiles and tears—
I am... th' Parson's Toilet!

Th' Parson's Toilet
(AN ODE TO THE INDOOR PLUMBING ROOM OF THE FORMER PASTORIUM OF THE FIRST METHODIST CHURCH, WINDER, GEORGIA.)

Long time ago they built this place,
and I was left outside,
But, with a half-moon on my door face,
I was still right full of pride.

Then, conversation in this town
said, "We're behind the times.
We just can't let our Parson down
to save a few thin dimes.

So, a committee set about
to try to find a place
to bring this room inside from out
and save the church's face.

There were no closets anywhere—
so ,where else could they find?
And then, that place beneath the stair
just jumped into their minds.

We'll build a wall right mid the boom
of that old open staircase
to close it off from the front room,
that sure will be a fine place.

City Slicker

A "City Slicker" is a guy
what knows more'n you and me.
He knows 'leventy million reasons why
we are dumb as we can be.

He thinks his education
makes him higher than the rest;
and he can run our nation,
'cause he knows just what's best.

He don't need no country bumpkins—
and, fer shore, no "religious right"—
to help him stand fer something
and keep his goals in sight.

Well, Mister City Slicker,
I can speak only fer myself,
but it seems the end comes quicker
when you bring it on yourself.

And, following your newfangled ways,
we have lost so many things:
like the meaning of our holidays,
prayer in school and our cause to sing.

So, please excuse me if I seem
not the least bit impressed!
Let's go back to the founder's dream—
"In God we trust" is best!

Their genetic tendency is just as strong
and the law of gravity helps them along.
I've thought both long and hard. I've asked both sage and bard
why they must fall down in my yard where they don't belong.

Not one of them has ample answer to my problems.
If someone knows a simple way by which to solve them,
tell me, for goodness sake! In the meantime, grab a rake.
We will sweep until we ache trying to absolve them.

Annual Migrations

The life cycle of the salmon is unique.
Revered and fabled is the one of which I speak.
Who knows the reason why it seems written in the sky:
they spawn—and then they die with much mystique?

Drawn by strong genetic urge, they swim upstream
despite dams and current's surge, they're on the beam.
Overcoming great odds, back to their roots they plod
in a way designed by God, to their spawning stream.

In jet-streams, they fly south ere winter comes.
In v-shaped line straight to the eye, they're going home;
back to their feeding grounds where plenteous food abounds
and icy mornings are not found, they are bound to roam.

When springtime comes, you see them flying north.
Rhythmic wings beat like a drum for all they are worth!
Duck and goose alike to their nesting places strike.
It's a sight of sheer delight for all the earth.

These annual migrations do intrigue me
and folk from every nation eagerly agree.
But one migration south, I could gladly do without:
when the leaves from all about fall from the trees!

A third time, the door flings open wide,
and in comes his favorite granddaughter.
Even Grandpa admitted he had too much pride
and loved her more than he ought to.

"Grandpa! Grandpa! Make a noise like a frog!"
Her sweet voice made Grandpa's mind slip a cog.

"Make a noise like a frog? Why in this world?"
Asked Grandpa with his mind in a whirl.

"Papa said," came the answer from his favorite girl,
<u>"When you 'croaked', we would go to Disney World!"</u>

When Grandpa Croaks

The door to the bedroom was slightly ajar
as Grandpa settled down for his nap.
Lately, it seemed he couldn't go far
before he ran plumb out of "zap".
Suddenly—wide-open—the bedroom door bolted.
From his afternoon nap, poor Grandpa was jolted.

"Grandpa! Grandpa! Make a noise like a frog."
Came the voice of an excited grandson.

"Go way, Son," Grandpa said in a fog,
"we'll talk when my nap is done."

Hardly had the door closed behind this one,
when it opened fast just like before.
This time, another young eager grandson
said as he raced through the door,
"Grandpa! Grandpa! Make a noise like a frog!"

But Grandpa just lay there like a log.
"Go way, Son! Can't you see I'm trying to sleep?"
Came the voice of a now irate grandfather.
As the boy from the bedroom started to creep,
he said, "That's my boy! Don't be a bother."

When she reached and took his bar tab,
Lindstrom knew he had a winner.
Then she said, "Let's call a cab
and I will take you out to dinner."

Satisfied with fine cuisine
and mesmerized by her charm and grace,
Lindstrom heard his fairy queen
say, "Let's have a nightcap at my place!"

The lovely night soon turned to day
and Lindstrom said, "I must go,"
after a breakfast that was truly gourmet,
"but there's one thing I have to know.

"Do you treat every man you meet this well?
And if so, I need to know why?"
"Of course not, silly. I think men are swell,
but you just happened to catch my eye!"

Lindstrom and the Redhead

Lindstrom eyed the gorgeous redhead
sitting near the end of the bar.
Visions of grandeur ran through his head,
but he didn't think he could go that far.

As he sat there on his bar stool
searching his mind for just the right tease
that would not make her think him a fool,
the redhead gave a violent sneeze.

Lo and behold, out popped her eyeball
and went sailing through the air.
Lindstrom, always good at baseball,
snatched it from its flight midair.

Now, he had the perfect cause
to approach this beauty rare.
So, without the slightest pause,
he handed her her eyeball there.

Profuse words of gratitude
issued from her luscious lips
saying she was in the mood
for company as she sat to sip.

SECTION IV

PHOOL-OSOPHICAL FANTASIES

JOKES, AND JUST PLAIN LIES

As with any other humor, rhyming humor is often based purely on imagination though, more often than not, there is a grain of historical truth embedded somewhere. Rhymes in this section are original by the author in their present form. Some of them are truly figments of his imagination, though some have their basis on other writings that are credited wherever possible.

Once when Quenchie, on one of his sprees,
just could not walk for the swaying of his knees,
his erratic driving a local policeman sees,
turns on his blue light, says, "Pull over, please,
but don't breathe my way—I'd get drunk from your sneeze!"
     It's off to jail for Quenchie.

When Quenchie woke up, his cell was locked tight.
He called to the jailer, "I know my rights!
I'm allowed one phone call. I ain't had sight
of a telephone. Nobody sleeps in this jail tonight!
I won't give up my rights without a fight—
     and on and on went Quenchie.

"I want to make a phone call!" he continued to yell,
banging on the walls and the prison bars as well,
He kept all the prisoners awake in their cells
until the change of shifts in the small city jail,
when a policeman came with a message to tell,
     "You can make your phone call, Quenchie."

"Don't want to make a phone call," Quenchie wailed.
A cop said, "You make a call, or I'll beat your tail!"
He thought, "There's no phone at home. Only reach us by mail
and none of my friends have cash for my bail!"
He dialed the phone, and said, "Send a cab to the city jail!"
     If you don't believe me, ask Quenchie!

Quenchie La Thirst

Let me tell you a tale about a family named "La Thirst."
The mama of this bunch was about to give birth
to a big baby boy who was surely not her first.
She thought about names from the best to the worst.
Said, "I'll choose one with which he will never feel cursed,
    I'll call him 'Quenchie!'"

"Quenchie La Thirst"—what a beautiful name!
That it had not been used before seems quite a shame.
I really do not know just who is to blame,
But our hero started out well ahead of the game
and the County of Barrow has never been the same—
    all because of Quenchie.

Quenchie never really liked having to go to school,
so, sometimes, he would "accidentally" fall in the pool.
He knew he would get home. Wet clothes were against the rule.
He thought he could use the principal as his tool.
After once or twice, prof. showed he was no fool—
    he had dry clothes for Quenchie.

When Quenchie La Thirst grew up a little bit.
He thought, "I've got the finest name a man could get.
I should do more to try to live up to it."
So, in spite of his mama's pitching lots of fits,
three or four times a week, he'd quench his thirst—get lit—
    all because his name was Quenchie.

Just at that moment of unfettered glee,
from his sleep he was caused to slip
by the departure of his wife, as she
went to the bathroom for her nightly trip.
Though still elated by his vivid dream
and wanting to make the feeling last,
he was seized by a terrible cramping that seemed
to draw him over double. It was gas.

Knowing his wife was out of the room,
it seemed a good time to let it pass.
So, he rolled over and let it go—Boom!
Such relief! He just hoped it would last.
As soon as his life-partner returned to the bed,
he flung back the covers to receive her;
then excitedly told of the dream that he had—
How they had been fishing together.

Repressing the trace of a smile on her face,
his sweet wife resignedly said,
"If we're fishing, cut the motor right at this place!
I think we're on top of a bream-bed!"

The Fisherman and His Wife

Fishing was a big part of the old man's life—
He was carried away with it.
It was not the same for his beloved wife:
for fishing, she cared nary a whit.
For all the years of their married life,
on every trip they took,
He would go fishing—but not his wife.
She went shopping, or just read a book.
Still, the old man longed for the time
when his shopping hours, she'd repay
by simply saying one little line,
"I'm going fishing with you today."

One night, as he was deep in his slumber
and playing on his field of dreams,
(which flitted by in unremembered number
and involved impossible schemes)
There was a vision of him in his boat
easing effortlessly through the canal.
There beside him, with rod, reel and float,
was his woman, his soul-mate, his pal!

And Prosecutor Kenneth Starr
does not seem to be too far
back in behind.

But Bill's a cool one under fire
and he's a most believable liar,
so he's not cornered yet.
Even with Monica and Paula Jones,
the chances that they'll pick his bones
are not an even bet.

Add missile sales and Asian money-
then throw in at least one more honey
who Bill thought was his type.
Of course, the nation's tongues will wag,
but there will be an empty bag
like when I hunted snipe.

Serious Thoughts

I sometimes wonder:
What does the President's under-
wear look like?

Does he ever worry
amidst all that scurry
and presidential hype,
saying, "I hope we don't have a wreck.
They'll see this ring around my neck
and know that it's not clean."?

Or, "Can they see my underwear
and see the hole that's under there?
They'll wonder where I've been!"

Or, "What would all those people think
if they knew that my feet stink
from athlete's foot infection?
Would they all still bow and scrape
and follow me through 'travelgate'
and hallow my directions?"

These and other serious thoughts
are like those often brought
forth in my mind.

He smiled a smile of heart-felt gratitude,
said, "Thank you, sir. I sho' 'nuff will."
Then came a subtle change in attitude
as answers to our questions he would fill.

"How many children have you?" asked my wife
He smiled and said, "Dey says I have fifteen.
I never has denied one in my life
as long as dey was nice and kept clean.

"Some fellows will deny and run away
like babies was bad as having rabies.
I figure it's just like dey always say
Dey's Mama's babies and Papa's maybes."

Mama's Babies

Roosevelt looked tense and insecure
as he sat bolt upright in his seat—
like he could not be completely sure
when he and great harm would meet.

His baseball cap was tilted very slight-
ly to the left, but spotlessly clean.
His eyes moved constantly from left to right,
back and forth as he surveyed the scene.

He did not seem to notice us at all
as we came in and sat in our chairs.
Two girls, one short, one rather tall,
acknowledged our presence with a stare.

Quite soon, the conversation started brisk
between us and these new-found friends.
But Roosevelt, not one to take a risk,
sat silently, eyes searching each bend.

The tenor of our speaking was quite light,
soon lead to the telling of a joke.
His change in expression was ever so slight,
but it seemed time to offer a coke.

The project was begun as she requested.
They even did some things he suggested.
Much time passed, and their patience grew thin.
Obviously, both of them were tiring.
When they found a problem with the wiring,
he was heard to mumble
as he grappled with conduit,
"If I could pull one nail without being told how to do it!"

A Family Project
OR TOO MUCH TOGETHERNESS.
(BASED ON A TRUE STORY THAT HAPPENS TO MOST OF US)

"That wall between the kitchen and the den
just seems to be a hindrance to us when
I am in the kitchen cooking dinner,"
she said as she began to plead her case.

"It seems to me, we would have more space
and all of us would end up as winners
if that wall were gone—torn down—erased.
I know we cannot spend much on this place,
but we can do the work and save a lot.

"Just think of all the time when we are not
together as a normal family
with the kids in school and both of us at work
Then, when we're all at home by some strange quirk,
that wall's between us. It doesn't have to be!

"I have some books that show how to do it
and both of us possess enough intuit.
It's something we can do and work together
on weekends and at night. It should be fun.
The hardest thing is to get it begun
and we can work regardless of weather."

Once again they braved the tide
and swam across to the other side.
What they saw there with eyes open wide
was a place that human taint denied.

Standing in the water's edge,
they gazed in awe upon the ledge.
Would stepping there be a sacrilege?
they pondered, and their minds would hedge.

No Coke bottles—no cans for beer
nor even human footprints appear,
but when they turned back to their rear,
the sign said simply, "Kilroy was here."

Spelunker's Surprise

Stew was quite fond of spelunking.
To explore a cave, he would go to Chungking.
Not that he was expert at the thing—
He just enjoyed the thrill it would bring.

Although his equipment was not the best,
he felt that he could stand any test
and was willing to join up with the rest
despite his parent's stern behest.

That a cave was there was all he would need
to saddle up his trusty steed
and to the cave mouth then proceed,
willing to follow or even to lead.

This cave was cold to make one shiver
when they came upon the underground river.
He dived right in without a quiver—
more brawn than brain for this free-liver.

Safely reaching the other shore,
the pair continued to explore.
To their dismay, they found once more
another river to be crossed o'er.

They hog the whole road like they owned the darned thing
and they seem to say, 'Aw, what the heck.'
Now me, I've been drivin' a car fer more'n 40 years,
and I ain't never had no wreck—no wreck,
I ain't never had no wreck!

Fon listened well and he took it all in.
then he thought it over fer a while
And he started to speak with that sly, sheepish grin
Fon often used fer a smile

And he said, with a twinkle in his eyes
now even a more sparkling blue,
"You and me, Mr. O., we're sorta' alike,
yet we're sorta' differnt, too—differnt too,
we're sorta' differnt, too.

"You and me both live in the same hick town—
me across the tracks from you.
My hair turned white—ha—yours turned loose—
it may be sad, but it's true—

And you drink your liquor from a crystal glass—
mine comes straight from an old fruit-jar—
And me, I've been driving a WRECK for more'n 40 years,
but I ain't never had no car—no car,
I ain't never had no car!"

The Ballad of Fon and Mr. O.

Mr. O. was the founder of the bank
and the chairman of its board.
Anything you could want that money could buy
Mr. O. could sure afford;

While Fon was a common laborer,
a saw-miller by his trade,
But when it came to doing work—or just raising cain—
Fon put the others in the shade—in the shade,
Fon put the others in the shade.

Fon and his wife had a car accident
both of them were hurt pretty bad.
Fon left her there in her hospital room—
come up-town—a-feeling mighty sad.

As he walked down the street fer to gain his strength,
just thankful to be still alive,
Who should he meet but our friend, Mr. O.,
who give him some words of advice—of advice,
who give him some words of advice.

And he said, "Fon, what's this I hear 'bout your havin' a accident,
Shucks, there ain't no sense a'tall in that.
People drive their cars down the road nowadays
like they had more lives than a cat.

All in the Family

The marriage was one that was made in Heaven.
It had really stood the test of time.
Both Willard and Jackie were past twenty-seven
and understood reason and rhyme.

In spite of all this, occasions arose
when they just failed to see eye-to-eye.
On such occasions, they could stand toe-to-toe
and words of real unkindness might fly.

It was such an occasion about trivial things
when tempers flared and got out of hand.
Words passed back and forth that made the ceiling ring,
with angry looks enough to beat the band.

The tone of the conflict reached such a height
you were glad neither had a knife or gun.
It went on too long—far into the night,
and neither one was having fun.

"I suppose you'll say you're going to your mother!"
She said, giving one last dirty look.
He said, "I am not! I'm going to YOUR mother!
I know she's a much better cook!"

SECTION III

PHOOL-OSOPHY

TRUE HAPPENINGS INVOLVING OTHERS... PERHAPS GARNISHED A LITTLE

Truth is truly funnier than fiction, if you are not put in position to laugh at yourself. Rhymes in this section report on real life happenings to family members and friends or acquaintances of the author. Some poetic license may have been taken in their reporting.

I'm better now. Those words have all come out.
My purging is complete without a doubt.
Therefore, my rhymings now should be
Living, vibrant, forthright poetry.
You think this makes a **poet** of me?
Then, <u>I've got this beach-front property.</u>
It's in Wy—

Purging of Archaic Words
AND FAULTY CONSTRUCTIONS FROM MY RHYMES

"Poetry that speaks a dead language is dead from its birth. . . .
When real poetry . . . is encountered,
 its speech is . . . direct, forthright, and living. . . .
—Clement Wood, <u>The Poet's Craft Book</u>

Methinks poetic choice they've run *athwart*.
'Twixt me and thee, a group of knaves they *art*.
To *abridge* our "poetic-shelf"
Of *chaps* and *gins* and *ye, yerself,*
Shouldst be *'neath* the *tricksy* of lowest elf
That *e'er wert*.

And *couldst ne'er we betake ourselves to* words
Like *wouldst* and *be'est* and *reft* is *plumb* absurd.
So *couch your lance*, join, if *thou wilt;*
We'll *lapidate* them *to the hilt*
'Til they *bedight* the *unlade* silt
That *liest* unheard.

Mineself doth oft bethink me of the past
How, *betimes, thine own self, wast rath*.
Since *I few battles fought* and won
By standing I, myself, alone,
And I ken well! *"Rath"* means "soon gone,"
I *abdicate*.

Almost every function a human performs
they assured me would get worse and worse.
There was nothing to do. It was only the norm.
Just a part of aging, man's curse.

I will never admit what predictions came true,
but one function keeps getting better—
improving each day and with all that I do.
That function is called my FORGETTER.

The wheels are in motion, the course has been set
and they're taking the one right direction.
When I get as old as the good Lord will let,
my forgetter should gain perfection!

Ode to My Forgetter

I'm not as young as I used to be,
but don't think of myself as old;
Though I'm not on the go quite as constantly
and my feet and backside get cold.

I've not had the failures of so many peers
who long ago slackened their pace.
I can still outdo some who are junior in years—
as long as it's not in a foot race.

When I was young, they said years advance
would cause body function decline
I would not have the need for as much romance
and would catch up quick when behind.

My vision would get fuzzy, my hearing poor;
my teeth would soak there in a glass.
I would not sing those high notes anymore;
My memory no longer would be first-class.

So many things they told me would fail.
I believed them for they were my elders.
My breath would be short and my step appear frail;
my hand shake when I would write letters.

Those clouds in the west look menacing
and threatening and frightening.
You know that more than anything
I'm deathly afraid of lightning.

The sun's rays are so hot that
I fear I might get cancer.
The mower's left tire is going flat
and our mechanic doesn't answer.

Since we had that soaking rain,
it's too wet. And let me state
that our neighbors might complain
if I mow the lawn this late.

There are many reasons not to mow.
My lawn shows I use them all.
Besides, if I just let it go
it will all dry up this fall.

Reasons Not to Mow

It's too early in the morning,
the neighbors will complain;
It's much too dry, my darling,
you know we've had no rain;

The weather is too hot
or it may be too cold;
Too young? I am not,
but I might be too old;

It is the pollen season;
the mower is out of gas:
All these are valid reasons
not to mow the grass.

Those grass seed need maturing.
You know there is a need,
if a lawn will be enduring,
to constantly reseed.

The falling yen is affecting me
and, also, the failing mark
(Meaning yen to work is low as can be
and I ain't got the spark.)

Tale after tale I could tell
about Papa and old Doc,
but hear me now—and hear me well—
this should not come as a shock,

Papa is a wonderful friend—
just like a brother to me—
and, when our lives here come to an end,
we'll tell tales through eternity.

We saw a little empty place
right behind that float,
though we were of a different race
and were pulling our boat,
we oozed right in like Jello
just as if it were planned,
and we rode through Monticello
accompanied by a band.

When Papa and I went anywhere,
the driving was done by me.
Having driven buses all those years,
Papa was quick to agree.
Then, when somebody would get sick,
old Papa was on call
because I didn't want to hit a lick
and Papa was having a ball.

Carlton had pneumonia—
was as sick as he could be.
I would make a house-call every day,
give him penicillin, three cc.
Papa carried in the medical bag,
said "In which hip do you want it?"
"Nair damn one," Carlton's faced turned red,
"if you are gonna give it."

Another time, we were hunting—
planned to be there all day long.
Each put a lunch in his bunting—
enough to feed a hungry throng.
Papa reached for his lunch sack
before the clock had got to nine
said, "I'd rather have it on my stomach
than to have it on my mind."

We were going on a fishing trip
to Florida's West Coast.
When from our duties we could slip,
it was what we liked to do most.
As usual, I fell behind,
and we got started late,
but the car was running fine
and making up time just great.

When we got to Monticello—
very much to our dismay—
a parade of all black fellows
was blocking our way.
Well, we were in a hurry!
We just didn't have the time
to wait for that last surrey
and fall right in behind.

Papa

Down South in the Peach State,
in a city known as Winder,
we all have the good fate
to know a guy who's a "stem-winder."
He did not go very far in school,
but he surely it not dumb!
Just try to play him for a fool;
watch out—your time has come!

His name is Morgan Mooney,
though I just call him Papa.
You might think I'm loony
 or telling some big whopper
when I tell some of the stories
that, I swear, are really true
of the deeds—not great nor glorious—
that me and Papa used to do.

We were somewhere north of Newnan—
 doing what, I do not know—
when we saw this ugly woman
whose face would stop a show.
Papa looked at this ugly barge
 (thankful she was not his spouse)
said, "How much would you charge
to haunt a six-room house?"

All they can do is lie there
awaiting God's final call.
I sure don't want to be there!
Not soon—if ever at all!

So I rise up on my pedals
and surge right on ahead.
Though it's a stern test of my metal,
I'm in no hurry to be dead.

Pulling Rose Hill

It may not seem like much to you—
no particular thrill.
It's something most any kid can do,
that is, pulling Rose Hill.

Rose Hill is not a mountain
where you can hardly see the top,
nor even a really sharp incline
at which all vehicles stop.

Rather, it's a gently sloping hill
about a quarter-mile long,
But it is a stern test of my will
to really see how strong
is my desire to exercise
and thereby improve my health—
knowing that is my only prize—
it will not increase my wealth.

I face Rose Hill each morning
as I first start my bike ride.
Then, as my muscles get to groaning,
I look on my right side
and see monuments to many friends
who did not make the pull
but came to an untimely end
before their time was full.

"Old Doc's done lost his license!
They caught him DUI!
Nothing else makes any sense!

Give me another reason why
He would be riding on a wheel
and parking in front of that place.
He just had to take a spill!
He just had to fall from grace!"

Well, friend, I hate to spoil your fun—
to rain on your party—
to be the loudest laughing one—
to play the part of smarty,

but as you see me pedal by—
looking somewhat like a rocket—
If you hear me laughing, you'll know why!
My license is in my pocket!

"It can't be true!" "Good exercise!"
"You set a good example."
"You really do take the prize"
are just random samples.

Encouraged by their kind words,
I resolved to pedal right on,
ignoring words I also heard,
"You'll die dead as a stone!"

I pedaled into Winder
to the office of the new Barrow Eagle.
It wasn't easy to find her—
had to hunt like a beagle.

When at last I found her
in the building with the DUI school,
I parked my bike in front of her,
a' feeling like a fool.

I wondered just how many fellers
would see me parking there
and put two and two together,
then go back home and swear

Just Pedaling Along

Every comment I could hear
said, "Man, you're looking fine!"
My weight up in the stratosphere—
my waist-line umpty-nine.

My blood just seemed to trickle.
I panted like an ape.
So, I started riding a bicycle
to try to get in shape.

It isn't easy for an old man
to exercise mind over matter,
but I had to do what I can
or just keep getting fatter.

My body didn't like it a bit!
My joints squeaked and moaned.
My mind said it's time to quit.
All my muscles groaned!

Most every head turned around
as down the street I "whizzed."
Conversation in the town
took on a strange new twist.

Each eye was glued on the preacher right then;
he faltered… then laughed a great roar.
He knew that bug would not try that again
as he lay deathly still on the floor.

The church aisle was filled with sinners that night,
not bound for the altar and correction.
After that tumble bug's untimely flight,
the preacher pronounced the benediction

I watched in great awe as a tumblebug
flew in through the window that night
and, as if he were pulled by some kind of tug,
headed straight for the overhead light.

Around that light in tight circle pattern
that bug flew. I followed with my head.
It reminded me of moons around Saturn
I had discovered in something I read.

Just watching that bug made me dizzy
as my head moved in its pattern of flight,
but I was not prepared for the tizzy
the bug caused that revival night.

After a hundred trips around the pulpit,
it zoomed toward the preacher's bald dome,
apparently needing to rest a bit –
but that slippery pate was not home.

The bug hit that slick head at full speed,
skidded off, and laid in the aisle.
The poor preacher felt a great need
to keep a straight face, and not smile.

The Flight of the Tumblebug

The church was not air conditioned
as none of them were in those days.
The members were all positioned
for a time of revival and praise.

The windows were propped wide open
to let air in and preaching out
in hopes passerbys filled with sin
would hear and be saved from their doubts.

The choir sounded just like the angels
as they sang *"The Jericho Road."*
My boyish, short legs seemed to dangle
in rhythm that I hoped never showed.

The evangelist stood in the pulpit
so soon wiping sweat from his brow.
I knew when he really got with it
he would be sweating a lot worse than now.

The old school globe light hung above him
centered behind his bald head,
reflecting quite bright from his scalp's skin
that seemed to glow, shiny and red.

"After him and Sis got married,
it didn't take Sister long
to notice all that stuff he carried
off, and figure, 'Sumpin's wrong!'
Well, she learned sumpin', Honey—
the biggest shocker of her life!
On the other side of the county,
he had several more kids and a wife!"

What she said did not surprise me.
I had heard it long before.
But, one thing she did not apprise me—
"Life or death?" For sure?
Struggling hard for a good answer
and, on my face, falling flat,
I said, "I don't see why your sister
keeps putting up with that."

"Oh, she ain't the one puttin' up with it,"
came her final sad outburst,
"The other woman's puttin' up with it—
He was married to her first.

Who's Putting Up with What?

There seemed to be an urgency.
She panted for her breath.
"I must see doctor immediately,
it could mean life or death!"
Her request, of course, was granted
without a needless delay.
I asked, "Why are you frantic?
What is the problem today?"

"Doctor, I wanna talk about my sister.
She's a'havin' a real hard time.
That man she's married to, Mister,
he ain't hardly worth a dime.
He ain't the good, fine man and husband
what he's got you fooled to think.
Jest 'cause he's got a little farmland
and he don't smoke and drink
don't mean that he's no kind of angel
with a halo 'round his head.
You just listen! Let me tell
why I wish that man was dead!

My effort to convince my mother to desist
was not the simplest task I ever undertook!
I felt quite certain I'd be at the top of her list
if she would let me see her little black book.

The reason I am sharing this funny little tale
is to impress upon all Baptist men and women
that whenever God calls, there is no need to fail.
Put mind and body to work, and your faith in Him.

Don't take "no" for an answer. Look for another way
when something comes along your action plan to hinder.
I don't know how many times I heard Miss Rosa say,
"When God closes a door, He leaves an open window!"

This business did not bother the nursing home too much
and never would, alone, have caused such great commotion.
Miss Rosa's second business was what brought on the fuss
and "must be stopped," they said with great emotion!

My mother keenly noted the pride most ladies took,
though in a nursing home, in their personal appearance.
She would bring out her mirror, so they could take a look
at ugly hair of which there should be clearance!

"I'll gladly take them off for only twenty-five cents!"
Miss Rosa would tell them as she made her business offer.
Quickly they would pay her, unless all funds were spent,
and Lottie Moon was richer by a quarter.

Miss Rosa would then take the large bottle of Nair
she'd ordered for herself right from the pharmacy.
Dipping a Q-tip, she'd work at the base of the hair
and soon that spot was slick as it could be.

This worked very well until she made the mistake
of removing hair from a diabetic's lip.
A fairly heavy rash made its ugly outbreak,
then from the bag that cat did surely slip.

Slowly she adapted to the nursing home routine,
and we thought surely she'd forgotten Lottie Moon.
She never mentioned it—though her mind was sometimes keen—
and we found we were wrong, but not very soon.

Everything ran smoothly until the phone call that day
from the administrator of the nursing home.
"We've a problem with Miss Rosa," I clearly heard her say,
"We need your help! How quickly can you come?"

Nearly sick with worry, I scurried the short drive
from my office to the nursing home's back door.
On my arrival there, when ushered to her side,
she seemed more angry than I'd seen before.

The problem that we faced stemmed from Lottie Moon
and businesses my Mother ran for the offering.
A public telephone was just outside her room
which, when someone would come a friend to ring,
Miss Rosa would announce, "Use my phone for a dime.
To use that telephone, you will have to pay a quarter!"
It seems this sales approach worked almost every time,
and Lottie Moon got ten cents for her larder!

So, for many years, beginning the first of January,
Miss Rosa made and sold her myriads of things.
She might attempt a sale right in the sanctuary
or to your home, the item she might bring.

She consigned her goods for grandkids all around
to sell. They said, "Yes, Ma'am," just like she was the Sarge.
It's quite needless to say, where such efforts abound,
each year, her Lottie Moon offering was large.

Long before her time, Miss Rosa showed some signs
of that dread ailment most folks call Alzheimer's.
It progressed rapidly with the erasing of her mind,
and she was forced to depend on her neighbors.

She was unwilling to consider living with her kids
and said she'd do quite well if simply left alone.
It took scary things before she recognized her skid,
and finally agreed to the nursing home.

We tried to provide for each and every need
and had a telephone placed right there in her room.
With those arrangements made, a pharmacist agreed
to send her needed sundries and perfume.

Miss Rosa and the Lottie Moon Offering

Everywhere we lived, my mother would soon be
president of the Women's Missionary Union.
It seemed as natural as the Englishman's tea
or Baptists still accused of closed communion.

She worked very hard to meet local needs—
and yet the real, deep longing of her heart of hearts,
was to help the ones who gave the spiritual feed
to heathen in earth's uttermost parts.

Miss Rosa knew quite well she never could be sent.
(Twelve children had long since shut closed that door.)
But, down in her heart, she'd never felt that meant
there was NO way she'd reach some distant shore.

One day she heard, with great surprise and joy, of the
"Lottie Moon Christmas Offering for Foreign Missions."
"Thank God!" she fairly shouted, her heart alive with glee,
"I've found the way that meets all my conditions.

Now, I can stay home, look after my little ones
and have my money sent to those who serve us here.
I can bake pies and cakes and make cute little aprons,
and sell them to my people everywhere!"

Pulling on his overall strap –
the bib filled to the brim—
like one caught in an iron trap,
he rocked forward and back again.

Finally, he caught his wind,
and started with these words,
"Tell me, where do I begin?
This is something I ain't never heard!

I never heard us Deacons was s'posed
to take care of the <u>people!</u>
The Church's business was all I knowed –
from the pews up to the steeple!

Miss Rosa's taught old Fred Seaforth,
and in my craw, it's stuck!
You can bet your boots, from this day forth
I'm either gonna DEAC or DUCK!"

"I plan to tell you how and when
your Deacons' work got started.
The church, like now, had problems then,
 so much they almost parted.

Greek widows felt they were done wrong
as the church gave food and drink.
The twelve apostles, felt as strong
that their preaching must not shrink,
said, 'Choose from among you seven men,
honest and of good report,
that we might put those seven then
over all work of this sort!'

"The church then chose those seven men
 and asked them to be <u>servers!</u>
The job's the same now as it was then.
 Will YOU be a deserter?"

Miss Rosa turned and took her seat,
having already said her piece.
The chairman rose up to his feet,
 tears ran down his cheek.

Miss Rosa showed up early
so she wouldn't miss a trick,
her Bible (with its pages curly)
turned to Acts Chapter 6.

The chairman called for order
and a Deacon read the charge.
They seated a recorder
and a prosecutor-at-large.

Miss Rosa boldly took the stand
at the time for her to speak.
Her voice seemed to be really grand –
not the least timid nor weak.

"I hear you men my saying begrudge
'Our Deacons fail to do their job.'
Before you come tonight to judge,
hear from the Word of God!"

Then she read with resonance
Acts 6, verses one through seven,
How the first church picked men as <u>servants</u>,
 after making prayers to Heaven.

"Our old cow just up and died.
There's no food for the kids!"
That day, somehow, a cow arrived.
It was things like that she did.

BUT

That was not her heart of hearts!
What really turned her on
was to exceed by far "her part"
for missions far from home!

"If our Deacons did their job,"
she was heard one day to mention,
"We could help Jane, Jim and Bob
and others in <u>foreign</u> missions."

Soon the Deacons heard about
Miss Rosa's stern conclusions,
and said, "We'll just throw her out,
for causing church confusion!"

Every pew was occupied
in the Baptist Church that night.
Men sat on the left side,
while the women sat on the right.

Miss Rosa and the Deacons

She was Baptist to the bone!
Her bone was Baptist, too!
She accomplished more alone
than most large groups could do.

They always chose her president
of the Women's Missionary Union.
What she said, she really meant –
let there be no confusion.

Called "Miss Rosa" all the same
by church sisters and brothers.
I knew her by her <u>proper</u> name.
She was always "<u>Mother</u>!"

Effects of the great depression
were quite evident everywhere.
It was not just an expression,
"I haven't a thing to wear!"

Miss Rosa was like a roaring fire
when someone had a need.
There were few days that would transpire
and her not do some good deed.

Just as soon as I got over my rash
(which took a week—or was it two?)
I was right back courting—but not quite as brash,
having learned the lesson that was due.

As a country doctor, treating all the ails of men
from a heart attack to a simple nose that runs—
every time I'd see a patient with an ivy rash again,
I'd say, "You remind me of Jane Dunn."

But, before the time we decided to part
and each go our own separate way,
I really loved Jane with all of my heart.
I toted home her books every day.

I did all those things a fellow should do
to greatly impress his best girl.
I'd jump a barbed-wire fence or two—
I'd chase a black snake or a squirrel.

I'd wade in the creek plumb up to my knees
to catch a crayfish or a lizard.
Never mind a cold or a little sneeze—
had to make Jane think I was a wizard.

One day, as I was flitting to and fro
on each side of the path that we took,
paying little attention to where I might go,
Jane hollered loud, "You'd better look!

That stuff that's growing up the side of that tree
ain't nothing but old poison ivy."
Grabbing a handful, I said, "It don't bother me."
As I rubbed those leaves all about me.

Remembering Jane Dunn

Jane Dunn was just the kind of girl
any red-blooded boy would like to know.
The kind you would give your best top that whirled
to take to be moving picture show.

I courted Jane right early in my life
long before I took up any cause.
I wasn't thinking about getting a wife.
I still believed in Santa Claus.

Jane would try to change all that stuff
before our courtship was through.
I guess I might have treated her rough
when she told me it just wasn't true
that some old fellow dressed in a red suit
would tumble right down our flue
without a single trace of dirt or soot
just to leave me a toy or two.

I got angry! No... downright mad!
I gave her a piece of my mind.
I told her if she was really that bad
another fellow she could find.

Fifty-two pictures of a nose spread everywhere
that still earns me the nickname of "Red."
Fifty-two pictures for twelve bucks plus tax.
Just hang them up high in the sky,
When garden time comes, you can just relax—
right over your garden those birds will fly!

Fifty-two pictures to grace your bathroom!
Don't put them face down on the floor.
They'll come in right handy! You know, I assume
that Sears doesn't print a catalog anymore!

To the Publisher

I spoke with you, Sir, a few days ago
about the progress our paper has made.
I asked if circulation continues to grow
and what plans for the future were laid.

You launched into some of your grandiose schemes
for both circulation and advertisement.
You shared with me your hopes and your dreams,
then asked if I had some advisement.

I told you I would give the matter some thought
when I had time for quiet cerebration.
I promised I'd share any idea time brought
to make our paper the best in the nation.

Well! I have sat down and mused quite a bit
and (I'm sure my readers will agree)
the best reason to subscribe to The Eagle is—it
would give you fifty-two pictures of me!

Fifty-two pictures of a face that shows some years,
yet the image was not made in recent past.
Fifty-two pictures of two eyes that have known tears
yet laughter would not allow those tears to last.
Fifty-two pictures of short, unruly, white hair
covering a knotty, oversized head!

Our path took a curve 'round the old stove-wood pile
and would frost in the Winter's cold blast.
I slipped in the curve, cut my head on the anvil
when we lived in five rooms with a path.

Perhaps that's the cause for my feelings to canker
so my soul just no longer hath
the slightest desire nor the smallest hanker
to live in five rooms with a path.

Five Rooms with a Path

Return with me now to the days of yore
when people took a weekly bath.
Our family was what we would call "dirt pore,"
and we lived in five rooms with a path.

Six boys and six girls with our Mom and our Dad
were crowded—you do the math.
We didn't know better, so it didn't seem bad
to live in five rooms with a path.

One girl wasn't born, and one boy had died
and one girl her own husband hath.
So, nine kids and our parents were living inside
when we lived in five rooms with a path.

A cyclone had struck and our old "two-holer'
lost its roof in the aftermath.
Then Summer seemed hotter and Winter much colder
when we lived in five rooms with a path.

We'd run down the path in a right steady jog
when green-apples exerted their wrath,
and would wish as we read Mister Sears' catalog
when we lived in five rooms with a path.

SECTION II

PHOOL-OSOPHY

TRUE HUMOROUS HAPPENINGS...
TO OR IN SOME WAY INVOLVING THE AUTHOR...
POSSIBLY GARNISHED A LITTLE

Truth is often stranger and funnier than fiction. The rhymes in this section relate to true happenings in the lite or experience of the author.

Some poetic license may have been taken, but in the main, they are truthful reports of live events.

Philosophy or "Phool-Osophy"

I'm a dichotomy! I'll bet you are, too.
I never know which side will show through.
Will it be the deep side some call philosophy?
Or the silly, shallow side I call "phool-osophy?
It doesn't really matter, for both sides are me!
I'm as much one as the other. I guess, I'll always be.

At one time or other, both sides served me well.
Philosophy has led me to more heights than I can tell;
but "phool-osophy" lifts me from depths when I'm down.
There is nothing more relaxing than acting like a clown.
Just which is the real me, and which the alter-ego?
What makes me click? What really makes me go?

I don't have the answer on the tip of my tongue.
"Phool-osophy" seems evident as when I was young.
But philosophy keeps growing, claims more of my time,
and I'm left to wonder the reason and rhyme?
Do I have to choose one? Or might it just be
that God, Himself, made me a dichotomy?

Solomon, that wise man said, "A time for everything!
For weeping or mourning—for laughter and dancing."
So, perhaps there is reason for a mix of the two,
hoping, at the right time, the right one comes through.
God help the man who no humor ever sees,
And help him who tries to live by just "phool-osophy!"

SECTION I

FIL-OSOPHY OR PHOOL-OSOPHY

Philosophy (I distort the word to Phool-osophy for humorous thought) has been defined as "the love or pursuit of wisdom." The wise King, Solomon tells us in the book of Proverbs to seek after wisdom, and he repeats that theme over and over. He also informs us that "a merry heart doeth good like a medicine." (Proverbs 17:22) and, "He that hath a merry heart hath a continual feast.

Phool-osophy is my word for those rhymes designed mostly to entertain. I see no real problem with offering both Fil-osophy and Phool-osophy in the same volume despite James' probing question, doth a fountain send forth in the same place sweet water and bitter?"

There is no designed bitter water here, only desire to make the heart a little more merry and to share a few pearls of wisdom gleaned in more than a half-century dealing with the physical, emotional and spiritual aspects of the health of human beings.

I'm not a poet. I'm a rhymer, at best.
Someday, when I stand my final test,
I'll stand before One at the great white throne
to account for the deeds that I have done.
Each thought I've had will be brought to light,
each word I've said, be it wrong or right.
I'll confess to the One who will judge me then,
"I never was a poet. Wish I could have been."

I'm Not a Poet

I'm not a poet—it's so much worse.
I see the whole wide world in verse.
No. I don't mean it's upside-down
or left is right, and so around.
I think God made this world, and time,
with a sense of meter and of rhyme.
Wherever I look, I plainly see
the handwork of God—His poetry.

I'm not a poet. I can't find words
to set hearts singing like mockingbirds.
It seems when I try to bare my heart
my words don't picture what I want to impart.
Things of great beauty clearly seen in this world,
like a mother and baby or a boy with his girl,
never show clearly in words used by me.
Though they usually rhyme, they're not poetry.

I'm not a poet. As hard as I try,
my words don't warm like a lullaby.
That elusive essence true poets possess
is just that, *elusive*, and I can guess
will continue to escape me 'til the end of time
unless God breathes spirit in my simple rhymes,
causing them to blossom and some soul to bless
with courage and conviction or…just quietness.

DISCLAIMER

To me, poetry has an ethereal quality that is seldom attained. It is not often didactic, rather it usually contains a subliminal message that leaves you wishing for more, while yet probing for its deeper meaning.

My writings do have qualities of rhyme and meter, but they lack sublime, ethereal qualities. They are straightforward and didactic, intended to instruct, inform, and/or entertain. I call my writings strictly "rhymes."

If, after reading, you should choose to call them "Poetry," and me, therefore, "a Poet," I am grateful and honored. In the meantime, I stick with my disclaimer statement,

"I'm Not A Poet."

Spelunker's Surprise 61
A Family Project 63
Mama's Babies 65
Serious Thoughts 67
The Fisherman and His Wife 69
Quenchie La Thirst 71

Section IV: Phool-Osophical Fantasies 73
Lindstrom and the Redhead 74
When Grandpa Croaks 76
Annual Migrations 78
City Slicker 80
Th' Parson's Toilet 81
The Complete Ballplayer 83
Lindstrom's True Friends 85
A Friend in Your Need 87
The Power of Scripture 88
On Losing the Weight Battle 89
A Pastoral Visit 91
Cruel and Unusual Punishment 93
Kiss My Canary 95
My Wife and My Girlfriend 97

CONTENTS

Dedication 7
Foreword 9
Disclaimer 13
I'm Not a Poet 15

Section I : Fil-Osophy or Phool-Osophy 17
Philosophy or "Phool-Osophy" 18

Section II : Phool-Osophy 19
Five Rooms with a Path 20
To the Publisher 22
Remembering Jane Dunn 24
Miss Rosa and the Deacons 27
Miss Rosa and the Lottie Moon Offering 32
Who's Putting Up with What? 37
The Flight of the Tumblebug 39
Just Pedaling Along 42
Pulling Rose Hill 45
Papa 47
Reasons Not to Mow 51
Ode to My Forgetter 53
Purging of Archaic Words 55

Section III : Phool-Osophy 57
All in the Family 58
The Ballad of Fon and Mr. O 59

As you enter the pages of *Fil-Osophy/Phool-Osophy,* you will find arranged according to subject matter, a few of his rhymed and metered writings that instruct, exhort, reassure and/or entertain. It is my hope they will mean as much to you as they have meant to my subscribers over the years.

Myles Godfrey
Publisher
The Barrow Eagle

FOREWORD

I feel much like A Godfather at the birth of *Fil-Osophy/Phool-Osophy*. I know its roots and have watched it slowly develop over the fire-plus years of my close association with its author. Never did I dream a book of poetry would come from any publication where I was in charge. You see, I had an almost ironclad rule against poems in publications owned or managed by me, and there were good reasons for that rule.

First of all, too many people try to write poetry, and too much of the poetry is bad. Then, all of these would-be poets are searching for a place to be published. My fear was that publishing one poem would open a floodgate of submissions (many from my subscribers), most of which would have to be rejected. Rejection of work into which these people have put their heart and soul is difficult for both the publisher and the author.

Only because of our friendship, did I take time to read his submissions when Doctor Skelton brought samples of his work and asked us to try him as a weekly columnist. I knew immediately that he was the exception to my "anti-poetry" rule. His writings were rhythmically metered and rhymed; Some were inspiring, some were touching. Best of all, some were hilariously funny.

From that day forward, I never published a newspaper that did not include one of Doctor Skelton's "rhymes."

He insists they be called "rhymes" instead of "poetry" because he makes no claim of being a poet. I say he can call them whatever he wants, but under any name, they represent some of the best writing it has ever been my privilege to publish, rhyming or not.

DEDICATION

God has truly Blessed me by placing female personalities in my life: one mother, six sisters, three wonderful wives (in natural succession) and five cherished biological daughters. Two great stepdaughters, and one daughter-in-law were bonus additions with my second and third marriages. Granddaughters and great granddaughters galore are now completing the picture.

Each has had a part in enhancing my life, causing me to see life's beauty more clearly, discern its philosophical moments more deeply, and appreciate its humorous aspects more fully. Because of their presence, their love, their actions and reactions, life has more meaning, more purpose and more hope.

> This book is dedicated to each of the aforementioned, but especially to the memory of my late first wife.
> **Nora Louisa Hart Skelton**
> and of my late second wife,
> **Hazel Marie "Penny" Morris Skelton**

These ladies have inspired, encouraged, consoled, cajoled, loved, cared for and gently driven me. Without them and their Christian faith (which enhanced and encouraged my own faith), my insights and perspectives would be much more limited than they are. My gratitude knows no end.

PHOOL-OSOPHY

A COLLECTION OF RHYMES ABOUT

HUMOROUS SUBJECTS

PHOOL-OSOPHY

A Collection of Humorous Rhymes

COVER DESIGNED:
SAM Y. MORIS

BY **DR. CB SKELTON**

ReadersMagnet, LLC

PHOOL-OSOPHY

www.ingramcontent.com/pod-product-compliance
Lightning Source LLC
LaVergne TN
LVHW011939070526
838202LV00054B/4721